CONSIDERATIONS ON FRANCE

JOSEPH DE MAISTRE

From a drawing by Vogel von Vogelstein

Joseph de Maistre

CONSIDERATIONS ON FRANCE

Translated by
Richard A. Lebrun

McGill-Queen's University Press

Montreal and London 1974

© 1974 McGill-Queen's University Press
International Standard Book Number 0–7735–0182–7
Library of Congress Catalog Card No. 73–84782
Legal Deposit 1st quarter 1974

Design by Peter Maher
Printed in Great Britain by William Clowes & Sons, Limited,
London, Beccles and Colchester

Contents

Preface

The present translation of *Considérations sur la France* is made from the critical French edition of R. de Johannet and F. Vermale (Paris: Vrin, 1936), which in turn is based on Maistre's own corrected edition of 1821. The critical edition also printed material that Maistre had struck out of his original manuscript. Where this material seemed to facilitate understanding of Maistre's thought it has been included in the footnotes. All Maistre's footnotes are reproduced, but with his Latin and Italian citations given in English translation. Latin quotations in the text have been allowed to stand, but English translations are provided in the notes. All added footnote material is distinguished by being enclosed in brackets. I have attempted to identify all persons, events, and references that might not be familiar to the modern reader.

I want to express my appreciation to Mrs. Janet Carroll, Professor Mark Gabbert, and my wife for reading the entire manuscript and offering a number of helpful suggestions, and to Mrs. Jean Birch for typing it.

This book has been published with the help of a grant from the Humanities Research Council of Canada, using funds provided by the Canada Council.

Introduction

The publication of *Considérations sur la France* early in 1797 announced the appearance of a formidable ideological opponent of the French Revolution. Just as Augustine had affirmed the providential governance of events amid the ruins of the Roman world, so Joseph de Maistre proclaimed that never had the role of Providence been more palpable than it was in the savage and bewildering events of the French Revolution.

Written and published in Switzerland, Maistre's book was vigorously prohibited in France. But the suggestion that irreligion had been the main cause of the Revolution proved attractive to many of its opponents. A providential interpretation of the Revolution made it possible to overlook social and economic injustice and similar factors less amenable to correction, and a return to religion seemed an understandable and traditional way of restoring order to the world. *Considérations sur la France* quickly established

Joseph de Maistre's reputation as an apologist of throne and altar.

He was born in 1753 in the Alpine city of Chambéry in what is today the French province of Savoy. In those days the province, though French in language and culture, was part of the Italian kingdom of Piedmont-Sardinia, and although he gained fame as an apologist for the Bourbon cause, Joseph de Maistre always remained a subject of the House of Savoy.

Maistre's father was a leading member of the local Senate of Savoy, a judicial body similar to a French parlement. Joseph was expected to follow his father in the legal profession, and he was, in his own words, 'delivered early to serious and thorny studies'.[1] His well-educated mother and his maternal grandfather, who was also a magistrate in the Senate, played important roles in his early education. After attending the local college he completed his legal training in Turin. He returned to Chambéry in 1772 and entered the magistrature.

There was little in Maistre's life in these prerevolutionary years to forecast the later publicist of reaction. Socially, the family must be classed among the upper bourgeoisie. Joseph de Maistre's paternal grandfather had been a cloth merchant in Nice. His father had come to Chambéry in 1740 and had advanced by talent and hard work. He was finally granted the title of count in 1778 in recognition of his considerable contribution to the codification of the laws of the realm. Joseph served with his father on commissions involved in the modernization of property laws; against the opposition of the older landed nobility, the reforming magistrates pushed through changes that allowed peasants to redeem seigneurial dues.

1. Letter to the Chevalier de Rossi, May 1808, *Oeuvres complètes* (hereafter cited as *Oeuvres*) (Lyons: 1884–93), 11: 109.

During these same years Joseph de Maistre was also intimately involved with Freemasonry. From 1774 until after the outbreak of the French Revolution, he belonged to lodges in Chambéry and associated with Scottish Rite Masons in neighbouring Lyons. Through the Lyons group he became acquainted with 'illuminism' and 'Martinism', esoteric and mystical doctrines that Maistre himself later described as 'a melange of Platonism, Origenism, and hermetic philosophy on a Christian base'.[2] Maistre dissociated himself from the lodges about 1790, but he retained an interest in Masonry and continued to collect and study 'illuminist' literature.

At first glance this Masonic activity appears to be an unlikely background for a future Catholic apologist. However, these eighteenth-century clubs were often frequented by priests and bishops as well as Catholic noblemen. Maistre seems to have been attracted to Masonry for a number of reasons. In the first place, the lodges were the right place for an ambitious young man to make useful friends for the advancement of a career. They were also a place to discuss and work for social and political reforms, and in addition, Maistre saw the popularity of mystical ideas in the Masonic circles he frequented as a providential counterforce to the rationalism and irreligion of the times. A memoir that he addressed to the Grand Master of the Scottish Rite Masons of the Strict Observance in 1781 developed both these themes.[3] He suggested that the fraternity act as a kind of power behind the throne to enlighten and guide monarchs, and he also proposed that one of the goals of Masonry should be the reunion of the Christian churches.

For almost twenty years Joseph de Maistre continued his

2. *Oeuvres*, 12: 248.

3. *La Franc-Maçonnerie: Mémoire inédit au duc de Brunswick*, ed. E. Dermengham (Paris: Rieder, 1925).

legal career in his native town, attaining the rank of senator just on the eve of the Revolution. However, neither professional work nor Masonic activities exhausted his time or his energy. He remained deeply interested in his studies and devoted long hours to the acquisition of languages and to extensive reading in both classical and contemporary authors, including the works of the Enlightenment. He would eventually become a bitter opponent of the philosophes and their ideas, but he spent years studying their writings and he never doubted their importance. Voltaire, Rousseau, Montesquieu, Hume, Locke, Leibniz and company were to be cited more frequently in his works than any 'Catholic' authorities. Could it be that the very bitterness of his later attack on the philosophes is a measure of the attraction he had once felt for their ideas?

Maistre was a close and sympathetic observer of developments in France in the years immediately preceding the Revolution. He admired Necker and approved his attempts at reform. In 1788 he looked to the magistrates of the French parlements as the logical leaders of moderate reform equidistant from monarchical despotism and popular excess. He approved the parlements' action in forcing the king to call the Estates-General.

In 1789 Maistre was at first enthusiastic about the possibilities of regenerating the nation. He owned property across the frontier in France and may even have considered the possibility of seeking election to the Estates-General himself. But the news from Versailles soon disillusioned him. He was opposed to the joining together of the three orders, and by mid-June he was predicting that a 'deluge of evils' would follow such a 'levelling'.[4] However, it was the night

4. We have indirect evidence of Maistre's reaction to events in France from letters written to him by his friend, Henry de Costa. Costa de Beauregard, *Un Homme d'autrefois* (Paris: 1878), p. 83.

of August 4th that was decisive in turning him against the Revolution. By September of 1789 Maistre was thinking of writing against the Revolution. He read Burke's *Reflections on the Revolution in France* (1790) soon after it appeared and found that it reinforced his own 'anti-democratic and anti-gallican ideas'.[5] Alarmed by the spread of pro-French and prorevolutionary ideas in Savoy, he submitted memoirs to Turin offering advice to the government on how to strengthen its position. Ironically, because of his earlier associations with Masonry, Maistre was regarded as a dangerous innovator by the Turin government and his suggestions spurned.

When a French army invaded Savoy in September of 1792 Maistre fled to Piedmont with his wife and children. But he returned to Chambéry in January 1793, perhaps to protect his property, perhaps because Turin appeared reluctant to reward his loyalty by offering him a suitable position. In any case, he found that he could not support the new French-sponsored regime, and he soon emigrated to Switzerland, where he settled in Lausanne. By April he had begun a new career as a counter-revolutionary publicist.

Maistre's *Lettres d'un royaliste savoisien*, published between May and July of 1793 for clandestine circulation in French-occupied Savoy, called for continued loyalty to the House of Savoy. The four letters reveal the dilemma of purely political royalism in an age of democratic revolution. What reasons could one give an enlightened generation for

5. Letter to Henry de Costa, January 1791, *Oeuvres*, 9: 11. Burke was a Protestant who held no particular brief for papal authority, so it is not immediately apparent how he could have strengthened Maistre's 'anti-gallican' ideas. But judging from Maistre's later writings, he may have felt that the more extreme champions of the 'liberties' of the Gallican church had undermined all authority in France.

loyalty to traditional institutions? Maistre entreated his readers to 'learn how to be royalists'. He admitted that while 'formerly royalism was an instinct, now it is a science'. Praising the 'exalted loyalty' of earlier generations, Maistre complained that loyalty had now become a 'matter of calculation'. But his own appeal was precisely to enlightened self-interest. For the most part the letters were an apology for the wisdom and moderation of the Piedmontese monarchy's rule in the decades before the Revolution. 'Love your sovereign as you love *order* with all the strength of your intelligence', he concluded.[6] Surely this was the very rationalism that had repudiated the old order.

In 1798, after the publication of his *Considérations sur la France*, Maistre burned his manuscript of the *Lettres d'un royaliste savoisien* as a 'fruit of ignorance' composed at a time when he had 'not the least *illumination* on the French, or better the *European*, Revolution'.[7] Between 1793 and 1796 Maistre had adopted the providential interpretation of the French Revolution that gave the *Considérations* its appeal and importance.

Maistre was not the first to suggest a providential explanation of events in France. There was ample precedent in the Christian tradition for regarding such a catastrophe as the work of Providence, and many thinkers on the Right advanced providential interpretations of the French Revolution (the Abbé Barruel provides the best example).[8] Maistre was distinctive in the sophistication, force, and clarity with

6. *Oeuvres*, 7: 82–230.

7. *Les carnets du comte Joseph de Maistre*, ed. X. de Maistre (Lyon: Vitte, 1923), p. 127.

8. See Paul H. Beik, *The French Revolution Seen from the Right* (Philadelphia: American Philosophical Society, 1956), and Jacques Godechot, *The Counter-Revolution: Doctrine and Action, 1789–1804* (New York: Howard Fertig, 1971).

which he presented his theory. His interpretation saw the Revolution both as a divine punishment and as a divinely ordained means for the regeneration of France under a restored monarchy. This enabled him to condemn the Revolution and the ideas it embodied and, at the same time, to accept it as a necessary prelude to the confidently prophesied resurrection of the monarchy. The political dilemma of this Savoyard royalist found its resolution in a religious vision of redemption.

If we may accept the evidence of a piece that Maistre wrote to console the parents of a young man who had died in the war, he seems to have arrived at the essentials of this providential interpretation of the Revolution by August of 1794.[9] His political theory was maturing in these same years. From shortly after his arrival in Lausanne he had been working on *Etude sur la souveraineté*, which was intended to refute Rousseau's *Contrat social*.[10] The *Etude* was never published during Maistre's lifetime, but many of its ideas were incorporated into the *Considérations sur la France*.

The impetus to combine the above elements in the present work seems to have been the publication in May of 1796 of a pamphlet by Benjamin Constant in support of the Directory.[11] Constant had been living at Coppet, the Necker family estate near Lausanne, with Madame de Staël, Necker's daughter. Maistre had continued to respect Necker despite the fact that many émigrés condemned him as a symbol of constitutional monarchy. Maistre visited Coppet on at least one occasion during this period and took an immediate dislike to Constant, whom he characterized as a

9. 'Discours à Mme la Marquise de Costa', *Oeuvres*, 7: 234–78.
10. *Oeuvres*, 1: 311–518. On Maistre's critique of Rousseau, see R. Lebrun, 'Joseph de Maistre and Rousseau', *Studies on Voltaire and the Eighteenth Century* 88: 881–98.
11. See note 1, page 65, below.

'funny little man'.[12] It appears that his composition of the *Considérations* was partly inspired by rivalry with Constant.

The book was written between May 1796 and late February 1797, when Maistre left Lausanne for Turin. It was published at Basel under the supervision of Mallet du Pan, the famous Swiss publicist. The title page carried the imprint of London, 1796, although it did not appear until the spring of 1797. There were four printings of the original edition as well as a corrected edition by the end of the year.

The book's appearance was well timed. By 1797 many Frenchmen were thoroughly disillusioned with their Revolution. The high hopes of 1789 had been shattered by the violence of the Terror and the hardships of war. The Republic had been consolidated by the Constitution of 1795, but the government of the Directory, as the regime established by this constitution is known, lacked popular support. From the spring of 1796, when the radical conspiracy of Babeuf had been thwarted, the regime seemed to be drifting to the right. At the time Maistre was writing his book, it was becoming increasingly clear that the majority of Frenchmen might cast their votes for royalist candidates and the restoration of the monarchy. The elections held in March of 1797, just after the book's appearance, resulted in the return of royalist majorities to the two legislative councils. The possibility of a restoration appeared so likely that the Directors resorted to violence in the coup d'état of Fructidor (September 1797) to keep themselves in power.

When *Considérations sur la France* is viewed in this context it may be appreciated as a shrewdly conceived tract for the times. Maistre appealed to the growing disenchantment with the immediate past by highlighting the goriest

12. Letter to the count d'Avaray, 30 August 1797, in *Joseph de Maistre et Blacas*, ed. E. Daudet (Paris: Plan-Nourrit, 1908), p. 9.

incidents of the Revolution. Publicizing the most glaring weaknesses of the Directory, he attacked the regime's lagging support. Maistre sought to strengthen the trend of public opinion toward the possibility and desirability of a Bourbon restoration. The crimes of the Revolution and the failures of the Directory were contrasted with the stability and peace that would attend the restoration of France's legitimate government.

But Maistre's book was more than a clever piece of propaganda. Arguing his case in broad historical, philosophical, and religious terms, he raised issues of continuing importance. His powerful prose crystallized an interpretation of the Revolution and all its works that was eventually adopted by a great many Frenchmen. The book remained popular throughout the nineteenth century, going through some twelve editions (with eighteen printings of the 1845 edition), not counting its appearance in various editions of Maistre's collected writings. The contemptuous rejection of the Revolution that characterized the piece typifies the attitude of many French Catholic royalists through most of the period. Maistre's little book offers valuable insights into the origins and implications of this hostility. It thus deserves careful study both as an occasional piece and as a source document for nineteenth-century French intellectual, religious, and political history.

Maistre's opening statement, 'We are all attached to the throne of the Supreme Being by a supple chain that restrains us without enslaving us', should be compared to the opening line of the *Contrat social*, where Rousseau proclaims that 'man is born free, and everywhere he is in chains'. To Rousseau's concern about man's dependence on other men, Maistre responded that it was more important for man to recognize his dependence on God. This dependence he finds miraculously apparent in the events of the French Revolution. Mallet du Pan's observation about the Revolution leading men more than men leading the Revolution becomes the leitmotif of an interpretation that portrays the Revolution as providentially ordained for the punishment and regeneration of France.[13]

In the second chapter this providential interpretation of the Revolution is combined with a flattering appeal to French pride. Belief in a divinely assigned French mission goes back at least to the Crusades. The nationalism of the Revolution was in part a secularization of this old idea. The French were proud of their army and its magnificent victories against the anti-French and antirevolutionary coalition. Maistre astutely acknowledged these glorious achievements, including those of the Jacobins in mobilizing French resources to meet the external threat. He called, not for repudiation of past accomplishments, but for recognition of a higher mission that included the religious dimension that had been so important for centuries. A purified France could lead a 'moral revolution' in Europe.

When Maistre suggests that those who favoured the Revolution did so for morally reprehensible reasons, he is playing on the guilt feelings of all those who had been appalled by the violence unleashed in the upheaval. Similarly, his dramatic portrayal of the punishment the

13. Despite Maistre's use of Mallet du Pan's concept and despite Mallet du Pan's assistance in publishing Maistre's book, their interpretations of the nature and significance of the Revolution differ significantly. When Mallet du Pan spoke of the 'force of things' it was not in providential terms but in terms of the complex political, economic, and diplomatic circumstances that so often seem to place events beyond the control of individual statesmen.

French had brought upon themselves by regicide makes the most of Louis XVI's 'innocence'. The king's reign had indeed been mild, and the failure of his regime's reform efforts was a real tragedy for both the monarch and his realm. Maistre intersperses his imagery of punishment and rebirth with a number of acid and perceptive observations about the goals of the anti-French coalition and the foolishness of certain counter-revolutionaries. This surprising combination of exalted religious perspectives and very worldly political realism often characterized Maistre's writing.

If the Revolution was willed by Providence, 'the horrible effusion of human blood' it occasioned must be interpreted as an appropriate means for the redemption of the French, and this is the object of the chapter 'On the Violent Destruction of the Human Species'. Maistre's reflections on this repelling subject may be more comprehensible to us than they were to his nineteenth-century liberal critics. We, who can add the catastrophes of the twentieth century to Maistre's 'frightful catalogue' of bloodletting, have had plenty of time and ample reason to dismiss 'the dreams of Condorcet'. But for Maistre's contemporaries his meditations on the shedding of human blood must have seemed a shocking repudiation of all faith in reason and progress. And his 'justification' of all this suffering in terms of religious sacrifice was even less acceptable. In some ways, of course, this chapter may be seen as early Romanticism. One thinks, for example, of Géricault's famous painting, the *Raft of the Medusa*, with its lurid portrayal of human depravity. And there is also a note of Romantic subjectivism in the way Maistre justifies his 'conjectures'. 'If they are not true, they are good; or rather, since they are good, are they not true?'

The rhetorical question 'Can the French Republic last?' (chapter 4) focuses attention on the precariousness of the

Directory. Maistre seeks in the first place to disprove the theoretical possibility of a permanent republican government for France. His attempt to provide an 'arithmetical' demonstration from the laws of probability may strike us as curious, but his discussion of English history is more interesting. He is essentially correct in stressing the feudal origins of representative government and the role of royal initiative in the development of the English parliament. Note that Maistre has no quarrel with the existing English system; he simply denies that it exemplifies popular sovereignty or 'perfected' representative government.

The French representative system (as defined by the Constitution of 1795) is subjected to sharper criticism. The whole idea of sovereignty of the people is satirized by Maistre's calculation of 'the prodigious number of sovereigns condemned to die without having reigned'. He maliciously points out that 'nation' can be a 'wonderfully convenient word since one makes of it whatever one wishes'. If the people are excluded from the effective exercise of sovereignty by the French system, the question is reduced to a comparative assessment of the rule of the Directory versus monarchical rule.

Consideration of the Directory's origins brings Maistre back to the crimes of the Revolution. Characterizing the Revolution as 'radically bad', he argues that it is impossible for any durable government (let alone a republic, 'that form of government which less than any other may dispense with virtue') to emerge from immorality and corruption. But he sees irreligion as the 'great anathema' of the republic and devotes an entire chapter to the antireligious character of the French Revolution.

In this 'Digression on Christianity', as the chapter is subtitled, Maistre maintains that religion must be recognized as 'the unique basis of all durable institutions'.

Many historians would agree that the revolutionaries committed a political error in attacking the Church; the Civil Constitution of the Clergy provoked massive resistance which in turn contributed to the Terror. But Maistre was more concerned with the metaphysical and sociological implications of the repudiation of Christianity.

On the metaphysical level, Maistre argues that man cannot be truly creative unless he puts himself in conscious harmony with the divine Creator and acts in His name. Only in this way can man share in the Creator's power. But Maistre addresses sceptics as well as believers, and his idea may also be understood as a sociological principle. Human reason, philosophy, is essentially disruptive; if you want to render an institution strong and durable, *deify* it. Significantly, Maistre's historical examples are drawn from pagan antiquity and Islam as well as from Judaism and Christianity.

When Maistre views Europe's problems in this perspective ('the immensity of our needs and the poverty of our means'), he concludes that one must opt between two hypotheses: the appearance of a new religion or the rejuvenation of Christianity. Now the idea of a new religion to replace Christianity was becoming commonplace by the time Maistre wrote. Robespierre's Cult of the Supreme Being (drawn from Rousseau's proposal for a purely 'civic religion') is only the best-known example of attempts to combine rejection of what was regarded as an outworn creed with the social benefits of religion. Maistre was original in boldly agreeing with the new prophets in their diagnosis of the situation and then paradoxically using their prescription for the needs of the time as an apologia for traditional Christianity. He agreed that men were witnessing a 'fight to the death between Christianity and philosophism', but he remained confident that Christianity would emerge from the terrible ordeal 'purer and more vigorous' than ever. But Maistre tended to identify the survival of the Church with the restoration of the Bourbon monarchy. In his vision the royal coinage carries the device Christ Commands, He Reigns, He Is the Victor. The assumption that the monarchy was essential for the Church was to be held by too many nineteenth-century French Catholics.

Chapter 6, 'On Divine Influence in Political Constitutions', is a summary statement of the ideas that Maistre developed later in his *Essai sur le principe générateur des constitutions politiques et des autres institutions humaines.* In fact in the preface to the 1814 edition of this latter work, Maistre reproduced his points about God's 'rights' in the formation of governments with the following comment: 'Since 1796, the date of the first edition of the work we quote, it does not appear that anything has happened in the world that might have induced the author to abandon his theory.'[14] Modern political analysts would not use Maistre's theological vocabulary, but most would probably agree with his fundamental thesis that written constitutional documents are relatively unimportant for the operation of any political system compared to the effects of historical, cultural, and social circumstances. Maistre's quip about the Constitution of 1795 being made for man, rather than for the real world inhabited by Frenchmen, Italians, Russians, and Persians, became famous.

The next chapter applies this thesis about the 'trade of constitution-making' to recent French experience. It is easy for Maistre to ridicule the 'prodigious number of laws' passed by the French assemblies since 1789 and to claim that the Constitution of 1795 merely provides a paper facade for a 'highly advanced despotism'. North American

14. *Oeuvres,* 1: 231.

readers may be more interested in his remarks about the new American republic. His recognition of the democratic character of the colonial prerevolutionary experience was unusual for his time. And if his wager about the building of Washington seems a typical bit of reactionary folly, there is one sense in which Maistre's prediction was not far off. Washington did become the political capital of the new nation; but unlike Paris or London, it never became a financial, cultural, or industrial capital.

Maistre's long digression on the 'old French constitution' (chapter 8) is primarily of historical interest. His judicial background is quite apparent in this discussion. He relies upon a book written by ex-magistrates of the French parlements for evidence about the character of the pre-revolutionary 'constitution', and his portrayal of the roles of the monarch, the parlements, and the Estates-General is essentially that held by most eighteenth-century *parlementaires*. But there had been a long-standing dispute between the monarchy and the parlements over their respective powers. By refusing to register edicts they judged to be in violation of the fundamental laws of the realm, the parlements had claimed the right to share in the king's legislative authority. Despite the fact that the magistrates' opposition to the royal will was often a matter of protecting their own vested interests as nobles and hereditary office holders, they had won considerable popular support as opponents of royal 'despotism'. In any case, Maistre was mistaken in assuming that the magistrates' book had the émigré king's approval. Upon receipt of a letter disabusing him of this assumption, he added a postscript to the second and subsequent editions of his book. But interestingly enough, the postscript does not really repudiate the parlementary position. Maistre states that if the magistrates' book 'contains errors that I overlooked, I sincerely disavow them', but he does not admit that there were any errors in the book. He thus took his stand with the French magistrates as an apologist for limited monarchy and an opponent of royal absolutism.

Maistre's prophetic description of the coming counter-revolution (chapter 9) attracted considerable attention after the event belatedly came to pass some seventeen years later. Maistre himself bragged of its accuracy, claiming that he had predicted everything down to the first cities to declare for the Restoration. But perhaps it was not too difficult to single out cities like Bordeaux, Nantes, and Lyons. The first two were port cities whose commerce had suffered from the blockades of the revolutionary wars, and Lyons had endured a terrible punishment under the Terror. But was it clever rhetoric or gentle irony that led Maistre to introduce his prophecy with the line 'Let us leave theory and take a look at the facts'?

The 'supposed dangers of counter-revolution' (chapter 10) is a topic less susceptible to clever phrase-making, and here Maistre is forced to deal at length with such difficult problems as the disposition of confiscated property and possible vengeance against those involved in the Revolution. He argues valiantly (and well on many points) that none of these considerations should prevent the French from enjoying the blessings of a restored monarchy. But one suspects that his concluding bon mot about the counter-revolution being not a *contrary revolution* but the *contrary of revolution* carried more weight than his lengthy argumentation.

The last chapter is a curious piece of work in which Maistre uses David Hume's history of the English Revolution as a literal 'lesson from history' to demonstrate his own interpretation of the French Revolution. This pastiche of sentences from Hume will scarcely impress the modern reader, but one can still admire Maistre's audacity in thus utilizing the English writer he elsewhere judged to be the philosophe 'who employed the most talent in the most cold-blooded way to do the most harm'.[15]

Joseph de Maistre is remembered for his vehement opposition to the Revolution and its philosophy rather than for what he recommended. Despite the extravagance of some of his rhetoric, he really advocated nothing more reactionary than limited monarchy. He thought that an hereditary nobility should be recognized, but he also left considerable room for careers open to talent. He was an apologist for Roman Catholicism, but despite his later reputation as a theocrat, he never advocated a 'government of priests'. His later book, *Du Pape* (1819), would champion papal authority, but less as an end in itself than as a possible means of controlling temporal sovereigns so that states might avoid the two abysses of despotism and revolution.[16] Of course Maistre's proposals were circumscribed by his assumptions about religion, the nature of sovereignty, and the presumed divine sanction for papal authority, but it can be seen that what he was seeking for the papacy was a role analogous to the one played by the concert of Europe in the years after 1815.

Maistre was most successful in opposition. His critique of the naive assumptions of contemporaries who thought they could create new political societies a priori, for example, was a valuable contribution. No doubt there are obvious weaknesses in his analysis. His intense concern with what he regarded as the culpable errors of eighteenth-century philosophy led him to ignore other characteristics of the

15. *Oeuvres*, 4: 248.
16. *Du Pape, Oeuvres*, 2: 167–75.

revolutionary movement. Despite an abstract appreciation of the historical process of development, he failed to recognize that the French Revolution was as much the product of social and economic change as of subversive ideas or religious decay. Nevertheless, with his intelligent criticism of eighteenth-century thought, his theory of the divine origins of political constitutions (new in form, at least), and a style that was mordant and eminently readable, Maistre helped make conservatism an intellectually respectable political philosophy.

There is a great deal of irony in the influence of *Considérations sur la France* on Maistre's personal destiny. In the fall of 1797 the book cost him a post as a Councillor of State in Turin. Just when he was about to be named, a letter of congratulations to him from the émigré French Pretender's court at Blankenburg was intercepted by the French and published in the newspapers. Since Charles-Emmanuel IV of Piedmont was an ally of the French republic at this juncture, his government could not afford offending the French by appointing Maistre to a ministerial post. The work caused him embarrassment again in 1814 when he allowed a new edition to be published in France at the time of the Restoration. When Louis XVIII had to accept a constitution, Maistre's book appeared to criticize the king's course of action, and consequently when this great apologist of the Bourbons passed through Paris in 1817 he was snubbed by the restored monarch.

Something should be said about Maistre's career subsequent to the *Considérations sur la France*. Late in 1799 he was appointed to a high judicial position on the island of Sardinia, and then in 1803 he was sent as Piedmontese ambassador to the Russian court at St. Petersburg, where he served until 1817. It was in St. Petersburg that he wrote his other well-known works. These include the *Essai sur le principe générateur des constitutions politiques et des autres institutions humaines*, which was published in Russia and in France in 1814, *Du Pape* and *De l'Eglise gallicane*, ultramontane tracts published in 1819 after his return to Turin, and *Les Soirées de Saint-Pétersbourg*, a theodicy in the form of philosophical conversations. The latter work was not published until shortly after Maistre's death in 1821. Maistre's thought may also be studied in other minor works (mostly posthumous) and extensive published correspondence. His diplomatic correspondence from St. Petersburg is of particular interest for his views on Russia and Europe in the Napoleonic era.

There is some change of focus in Maistre's later writings, with more emphasis on general religious and philosophical questions, but his judgement of the French Revolution and its consequences for Europe never varied significantly from the views expressed in the *Considérations*. He was dissatisfied with the Restoration he lived to see, and he continued to fear the ultimate triumph of the forces he had so strenuously opposed. Not long before his death he wrote to a friend, 'I die with Europe, I am in good company.'[17]

17. Letter to the count de Marcellus, 9 August 1819, *Oeuvres*, 14: 183.

CONSIDERATIONS
ON FRANCE

I

Of Revolutions

We are all attached to the throne of the Supreme Being by a supple chain that restrains us without enslaving us. Nothing is more admirable in the universal order of things than the action of free beings under the divine hand. Freely slaves, they act voluntarily and necessarily at the same time; they really do what they will, but without being able to disturb the general plans. Each of these beings occupies the centre of a sphere of activity whose diameter varies according to the will of the Eternal Geometer, who can extend, restrict, check, or direct the will without altering its nature.

In the works of man, everything is as wretched as their author; views are restricted, means rigid, motives inflexible, movements painful, and results monotonous. In divine works, the riches of infinity are openly displayed in the least part. Its power is exercised effortlessly; everything is supple in its hands, nothing resists it, and for it everything, even obstacles, are means; and the irregularities introduced by the operation of free agents fit into the general order.

If we imagine a watch all of whose springs vary continually in strength, weight, dimension, form, and position that nevertheless invariably keeps perfect time, we will form some idea of the action of free beings relative to the plans of the Creator.

In the political and moral world, as in the physical world, there is a usual order and there are exceptions to this order. Ordinarily, we see series of effects produced by the same causes; but in certain epochs, we see actions suspended, causes paralysed, and new effects.

A *miracle* is an effect produced by a divine or superhuman cause that suspends or contradicts an ordinary cause. If in the middle of winter, before a thousand witnesses, a man were to command that a tree be suddenly covered with leaves and fruit, and the tree obeyed, everyone would proclaim it a miracle and bow down before the wonderworker. But the French Revolution and everything now happening in Europe is just as marvellous in its own way as the instantaneous fructification of a tree in the month of January. However, instead of being astonished, we look the other way or talk nonsense.

In the physical order, in which man does not play a role as a cause, he is quite willing to admire what he does not understand. But in the sphere of his own activity, where he feels that he is a free cause, man's pride easily leads him to see *disorder* wherever his action is suspended or disturbed. Certain measures that are in man's power regularly produce certain effects in the ordinary course of events; if he misses his mark, he knows why or believes he does. He knows the obstacles, he appreciates them, and nothing surprises him.

But in revolutionary periods, the chain that binds man is abruptly shortened; his action is diminished and his means deceive him. Then carried along by an unknown force, he frets against it, and instead of kissing the hand that clasps him, he disregards or insults it.

'I do not understand it at all' is the fashionable phrase. This is a sensible reaction if it leads to the first cause that is presently presenting so great a spectacle to men; it is stupidity if it expresses only vexation or sterile despondency. 'How then', they cry on every side, 'is it the guiltiest men in the universe who are winning? A hideous regicide succeeds as well as those who committed it could have hoped. All over Europe monarchy is benumbed. Its enemies find allies even on thrones![1] Everything succeeds for the wicked![2] The most gigantic projects are executed without difficulty on their side, while the good party fails ridiculously in everything it undertakes.[3] Public opinion persecutes fidelity all over Europe![4] The foremost statesmen are invariably mistaken![5] The greatest generals are humiliated! etc.'

1. [Probably a reference to the Prussian and Spanish monarchs who concluded separate peace treaties with France in 1795.]

2. [Perhaps refers to Bonaparte's Italian campaign of 1796.]

3. [Probably an allusion to such royalist fiascos as the 1795 landing at Quiberon in Brittany. This affair, much like the 1961 Bay of Pigs episode in Cuba, saw the complete defeat of a British-supported émigré invasion when the invaders failed to win the support of the local population.]

4. [Louis XVIII, Louis XVI's brother and the unacknowledged claimant to the French throne since the death of his nephew, Louis XVII in June 1795, was expelled from Verona by the Venetians in April 1796. Finding himself unwelcome in Austria, he finally found refuge in Blankenburg, in the Duchy of Brunswick. The Directory had requested the Swiss Confederation to expel the émigrés, and a number of German cities declared that they did not wish to receive them.]

5. [Probably a reference to William Pitt, since 1793 the leader of the anti-French coalition.]

Doubtless, for the first condition of an ordained revolution is that whatever could have prevented it does not exist and that nothing succeed for those who wish to prevent it. But never is order more visible, never is Providence more palpable, than when superior action is substituted for that of man and it acts all alone. This is what we are seeing at the present moment.

The most striking thing about the French Revolution is this overwhelming force that bends every obstacle. It is a whirlwind carrying along like light straw everything that human force has opposed to it; no one has hindered its course with impunity. Purity of motives has been able to make resistance honourable, but no more, and this jealous force, proceeding straight toward its goal, rejects equally Charette, Dumouriez, and Drouet.[6]

It has been correctly pointed out that the French Revolution leads men more than men lead it. This observation is completely justified, and although it can be applied to all great revolutions more or less, it has never been more striking than it is in the present period.

The very rascals who appear to lead the Revolution are involved only as simple instruments, and as soon as they aspire to dominate it they fall ignobly. Those who established the Republic did it without wanting to and without

6. [On 10 August, 1792, the day the monarchy was overthrown, Charette had tried in vain to rescue Louis XVI from the Tuileries; later he gained fame as a Vendée chieftain. Dumouriez, who was minister of foreign affairs in March 1792, did his best to provoke war with the Austrians in the secret hope that war would rally the French in support of their king. Later, in March 1793, as commanding general of the Army of the North he made an unsuccessful attempt to use his army to overthrow the Jacobins. Drouet, who was the postmaster at Saint-Menéhould in June 1791, recognized the fleeing Louis XVI and was instrumental in his arrest at Varennes.]

knowing what they were doing. They were led to it by events; a prior design would not have succeeded.

Robespierre, Collot, or Barère never thought to establish the revolutionary government or the Reign of Terror;[7] they were led to it imperceptibly by circumstances, and the like will never be seen again. These extremely mediocre men exercised over a guilty nation the most frightful despotism in history, and surely they were more surprised at their power than anyone else in the kingdom.[8]

But the very moment these detestable tyrants completed the measure of crime necessary to that phase of the Revolution, a breath overthrew them.[9] Their gigantic power, which had made France and Europe tremble, could not withstand the first attack; and as there could be nothing great, nothing august, in a completely criminal revolution, Providence willed that the first blow be struck by the Septembrists,[10] in order that justice itself would be debased.[11]

7. [Robespierre, Collot, and Barère were leading members of the Committee of Public Safety.]

8. [The original manuscript added, 'This despotism was a just punishment for a people who had desired liberty in a criminal manner and whose culpable efforts had led to the most frightful regicide.']

9. [Allusion to the events of Thermidor and the fall of Robespierre and his close colleagues.]

10. [Billaud-Varenne and Tallien, who had been ministers of the Commune of Paris at the time of the September massacres (1792), were among those who helped bring down Robespierre on 9 Thermidor.]

11. For the same reason, honour was dishonoured. One journalist (in le Republicain) said with much wit and justice, 'I understand very well how they can depantheonize Marat, but I will never understand how they will be able to demaratize the Panthéon.' Someone complained of seeing Turenne's body forgotten in the corner of a museum next to an animal skeleton. What imprudence! It was enough to give rise to the idea of tossing his

We are often astonished that the most mediocre men have been better judges of the French Revolution than men of first-rate talent, that they have believed in it completely while accomplished politicians have not believed in it at all. This is because this belief is one of the characteristics of the Revolution, because the Revolution could succeed only by the scope and power of the revolutionary spirit, or, if one may put it another way, by *faith* in the Revolution. Thus, untalented and ignorant men have very ably driven what they call the *revolutionary chariot*. They have dared everything without fear of counter-revolution; they have always gone ahead without looking back, and everything has succeeded for them because they were only the instruments of a force that knew more than they did. They made no mistakes in their revolutionary career for the same reason that Vaucanson's flutist never hit a false note.[12]

The revolutionary torrent took successively different directions, and it was only by following the course of the

---

venerable remains into the Panthéon. [The Panthéon was built as the Church of St. Geneviève in the decades before the Revolution. It was converted to a temple of fame (*pantheon* is Greek for a temple dedicated to all the *gods*) at the death of Mirabeau in 1791. It remains the place of entombment for France's national heroes. Marat, who was assassinated in July 1793, was interred in the Panthéon as a Jacobin martyr in 1794. By 1795 he had become a symbol of revolutionary excess, and his body was removed to a nearby cemetery. Turenne, one of Louis XVI's most famous generals, had been buried at Saint-Denis. When the royal tombs were pillaged in 1793, his remains were removed to the museum. The Directory decided to honour him, but he was never moved to the Panthéon. He was finally laid to rest in Les Invalides by Napoleon in 1800.]

12. [Jacques de Vaucanson (1709–82), a famous inventor, first attracted attention with an elaborate mechanical flute player that he displayed in Paris in 1737.]

moment that the most conspicuous men in the Revolution acquired the kind of power and celebrity they were able to achieve. As soon as they wanted to oppose it, or even to stand aside by isolating themselves or by working too much for themselves, they disappeared from the scene.

Look at Mirabeau, who was so conspicuous in the Revolution; at bottom he was only *the king of the market hall.* By the crimes that he committed and the books that he wrote he seconded the popular movement. He placed himself behind a mass already put in motion and pushed it in the already determined direction; his power never extended any further. He shared with another hero of the Revolution[13] the power of agitating the multitude without being able to dominate it—which in political troubles amounts to the true stamp of mediocrity. Rebels less brilliant, and in effect more able and more powerful than he, used his influence for their own profit. He thundered in the tribune and he was their dupe.[14] He said in dying that if he had lived, he would 'have reassembled the scattered pieces of the monarchy', and yet, when in the moment of his greatest influence he wanted only a ministry, his underlings pushed him aside like a child.[15]

13. [Lafayette.]

14. [Like many modern politicians, Mirabeau used a group of 'ghost writers', who wrote many of the speeches that he delivered in the Constituent Assembly. Since some of these writers were men of talent, wealth, and ambition (the financier Clavière, for example, who collaborated with Mirabeau on speeches on financial matters), the question of who was duping whom remains open. See O. J. G. Welsh, *Mirabeau* (Port Washington, N.Y.: Kennikat Press, 1968), pp. 211–12.]

15. [In late 1790 and early 1791, Mirabeau sought to organize a ministry that would halt the course of the Revolution. His fellow deputies and the king distrusted him, and consequently his schemes were stillborn. He died of natural causes a short time later.]

In short, the more one examines the apparently most active personages in the Revolution, the more one finds in them something passive and mechanical. We cannot repeat too often that men do not lead the Revolution; it is the Revolution that uses men. They are right when they say *it goes all alone.* This phrase means that never has the Divinity shown itself so clearly in any human event. If the vilest instruments are employed, punishment is for the sake of regeneration.

II

Reflections on the Ways of Providence in the French Revolution

Every nation, like every individual, has received a mission that it must fulfil. France exercises over Europe a veritable magistracy that it would be useless to contest and that she has most culpably abused. In particular, she was at the head of the religious system, and not without reason was her king called *most Christian*; Bossuet was never able to say too much on this point. And so, since she has used her influence to contradict her vocation and demoralize Europe, we should not be surprised if she is brought back to her mission by terrible means.

It has been a long time since we have seen such frightful punishment inflicted on such a large number of guilty people. No doubt there are innocents among the unfortunate victims, but they are far fewer than is commonly imagined.

All those who laboured to free the people from their religious beliefs, all those who opposed the laws of property with metaphysical sophisms, all those who said 'Strike, so long as we win something', all those who counselled, approved, or favoured the use of violent measures against the king, etc., all these willed the Revolution, and all who willed it have very justly, even according to our limited insight, become its victims.

We groan to see illustrious scholars fall beneath Robespierre's axe. Humanly, we cannot be too sorry for them; but divine justice has not the least respect for geometers or physicists.[1] Too many French scholars were the principal authors of the Revolution, too many approved and gave their support so long as the Revolution, like Tarquin's sceptre, struck down only the tallest heads.[2] Like so many others, they said, *It is impossible to make a great revolution without incurring misfortunes.* But when a philosopher justifies evil by the end in view, when he says in his heart, *Let there be a hundred thousand murders, provided we are free,* and Providence replies, *I accept your offer, but you must be included in the number,* where is the injustice? Would we judge otherwise in our own tribunals?

Details would be odious;[3] but there are few Frenchmen

1. [Maistre's original manuscript names Bailly, a mathematician and astronomer who became mayor of Paris in the first phase of the Revolution, and Lavoisier, a famous physicist who became politically suspect because before the Revolution he had been a member of a tax-farming syndicate. Both were guillotined during the Terror. The judge at Lavoisier's trial is said to have remarked, 'The Republic has no need for genius.']

2. [Tarquinius, an early Roman king, is supposed to have struck off the heads of the tallest poppies in his garden as an object lesson in how to bring about the submission of a rebellious city.]

3. [Maistre's original manuscript included a long digression on Malesherbes, who as director of publications had allowed the publication of the *Encyclopédie* and who later defended Louis XVI at his trial before the National Convention in 1792, an act which later led to his arrest and death by guillotine. Maistre blamed

among those they call 'innocent victims of the Revolution' to whom their consciences could not say

> Now see the sad fruits your faults produced,
> Feel the blows you have yourselves induced.[4]

Our ideas on good and evil, on innocence and guilt, are often affected by our prejudices. If two men fight each other with three-inch daggers, they are judged guilty and shameful; but if they use three-foot blades, the combat becomes an honourable contest. We brand someone who steals one centime from his friend's pocket; if he steals only his friend's wife, it is nothing. Brilliant crimes involving great or likeable qualities, especially when they are rewarded by success, are pardoned or even admired. But in the eyes of true justice, the criminal is blackened by his best qualities because his greatest crime is his abuse of talent.[5]

Every man has certain duties to fulfil, and the extent of his duties is relative to his civil position and the extent of his means. The same action on the part of two given men may be very far from being equally criminal. In the same way, an action that is only an error or a bit of madness on the part of an obscure man suddenly raised to unlimited power would be a crime if committed by a bishop, duke, or peer.[6]

Malesherbes for allowing the publication of the books produced by a detestable 'philosophic sect', but conceded that he had redeemed his honour by defending the king.]

4. Racine, *Iphigénie*, V, 2.

5. [The original manuscript continued, 'Voltaire, whom blind enthusiasts have placed in the Panthéon, is perhaps more guilty of the judgement of Divinity than Marat, for he may have made Marat, and he certainly did more evil than Marat.']

6. [Probably allusions to Talleyrand, who had been bishop of Autun, and to the duke of Orléans, a cousin of the king, who became known as Philippe Egalité for his role in the Revolution.]

And finally, there are actions that, though excusable, and even praiseworthy from a human point of view, are in essence infinitely criminal. If, for example, someone tells us, *I embraced the French Revolution in good faith, for pure love of liberty and country; I believed in my soul and conscience that it would lead to the reform of abuses and the public welfare,* we have nothing to say. But He who knows the hearts of men sees the guilty disposition; He discovers in a ridiculous misunderstanding, in a little rumpling of pride, in a base or criminal passion, the prime mover behind those resolutions that we would like to display as noble, and for Him the lie of hypocrisy grafted onto treason is an additional crime. But let us speak of the nation in general.

An assault against sovereignty is undoubtedly one of the greatest crimes that can be committed; none has more terrible consequences. If sovereignty rests on a single head and that head falls victim to the assault, the crime is augmented by atrocity. But if this sovereign had committed no crime meriting such an attack, if the guilty were armed against him by his very virtues, the crime becomes un-speakable. We recognize here the death of Louis XVI. But what is important to note is *that never has a greater crime had more accomplices.* Far fewer were involved in the death of Charles I, even though he merited some blame and reproach and Louis XVI did not. Nevertheless he was given proofs of the most devoted courageous concern; even the executioner, who was only obeying orders, dared not reveal his identity. In France, Louis XVI marched to his death surrounded by 60,000 armed men who had not a shot for *Santerre*;[7] not a voice was raised for the unfortunate

7. [Santerre had been the commander of the Paris National Guard since 10 August 1792. On 18 January 1793 (three days before the king's execution) he told the Convention, 'Everything is perfectly quiet; the sentence of the former king will be executed

monarch, and the provinces were as mute as the capital. We would expose ourselves, they said. Frenchmen! If you find this a good reason, talk no more of your courage, or admit that you have used it very badly.

The indifference of the army was no less remarkable. Having betrayed Louis XVI, it served his executioners much better than it had served the king. There was not the slightest testimony of discontent.[8] In sum, never have a greater number of guilty people shared (with many gradations, to be sure) in a greater crime.

We must make another important observation, which is that every assault committed against sovereignty *in the name of the nation* is always more or less a national crime, for it is always more or less the fault of the nation if any number of rebels can put themselves in a position to commit a crime in its name. Thus, no doubt not all Frenchmen *willed* the death of Louis XVI; but the immense majority of the people, for more than two years, *willed* all the follies, all the injustices, all the outrages that led up to the catastrophe of 21 January.[9]

Now all national crimes against sovereignty are punished without delay and in a terrible manner; this is a law that has never suffered exception. A few days after Louis XVI's execution, someone wrote in the *Mercure universel*, 'Perhaps it was not necessary to go that far, but since our

---

with the greatest array. There is presently a reserve of nearly five thousand men ready to march; there are cannons everywhere, but they are unnecessary. Tranquillity cannot be interrupted.']

8. [This is not entirely correct. After Louis XVI's flight to Varennes, the Constituent Assembly prescribed a loyalty oath for the army. About 2,000 officers out of 9,500 on active duty refused to swear it.]

9. [21 January 1793 was the date of Louis XVI's execution.]

legislators have taken the initiative on their own responsibility, let us rally around them, appease all hatreds, and forget the matter.'[10] Very well, it was perhaps unnecessary to assassinate the king; but since the deed is done, do not mention it again and let us all be good friends. Madness! Shakespeare knew better when he said

> The single and peculiar life is bound,
> With all the strength and armour of the mind,
> To keep itself from noyance; but much more
> That spirit upon whose weal depend and rest
> The lives of many. The cease of majesty
> Dies not alone; but, like a gulf, doth draw
> What's near it with it.[11]

Perhaps four million Frenchmen will pay with their heads for this great national crime of an antireligious and antisocial insurrection crowned by a regicide.

Where are the first national guardsmen, the first soldiers, the first generals who swore an oath to the nation? Where are the chiefs, the idols of that first guilty assembly for which the epithet of *constituent* will be an eternal epigram? Where is Mirabeau? Where is Bailly with his 'wonderful

10. [*Moniteur universel*, 23 January 1793. Maistre cites the title incorrectly. The journal concluded its account of the king's execution with the following comments: 'But let us leave Louis under the shroud; henceforth he belongs to history. For a moral and sensitive man there is something hallowed about a victim of the law. Now all good citizens must turn their wishes, their talents, and their strength toward the future. Divisions have made enough trouble in France. All honest men must sense the need for unity, and those who do not feel its attraction have still more reason for desiring its existence. A few principles, a little effort, and a coalition fatal to the wicked will be consummated.']

11. *Hamlet*, Act 3, Scene 8.

day'?[12] Where is Thouret, who invented the phrase 'to expropriate'? Where is Osselin, who introduced the first law proscribing émigrés?[13] One could name by the thousands the active instruments of the Revolution who have died a violent death.

Here again we may admire order in disorder, for it is evident, if we reflect a bit, that the guiltiest revolutionaries could be felled only by the blows of their accomplices. If force alone had accomplished what they call the counter-revolution and restored the king to his throne, there would have been no way of rendering justice. For a sensitive man to have to judge the assassins of his father, his relatives, and his friends, or merely the usurper of his property, would be the greatest misfortune that could happen to him. Now this is precisely what would have happened if the counter-revolution had occurred as expected. The superior judges, by the very nature of things, would almost all have belonged to the injured class, and justice, even if it merely punished, would have had an air of vengeance. Moreover, legitimate authority always retains a certain moderation in the punishment of crimes involving a multitude of accomplices. When five or six are put to death for the same crime it is a massacre; if punishment exceeds certain limits it becomes odious. In short, great crimes unfortunately require great punishments, and the limits are easily exceeded when it is a question of crimes of lese majesty, and flattery becomes the executioner. Humanity still has not

12. [When the king was forced to come to Paris on 5 October 1789, Mayor Bailly greeted him with the following words (no irony intended, apparently): 'What a wonderful day, sire, on which the Parisians have Your Majesty and his family in their city.']

13. [Except for Mirabeau, who died a natural death, these men, who were leading revolutionaries in the Constituent Assembly, were all guillotined during the Terror.]

pardoned former French legislation for Damiens's horrible punishment.[14] So what could French magistrates have done with three or four hundred *Damienses* and all the monsters who are overrunning France?

Would the sacred sword of justice have fallen relentlessly like Robespierre's guillotine? Would all the executioners and all the artillery horses of the realm be summoned to Paris to quarter men? Would lead and pitch be melted in vast boilers to sprinkle on limbs torn by red-hot pincers? Moreover, how would the crimes be characterized? How would the penalties be measured? And above all, how would there be punishment without laws? You say *that some of the guiltiest would be chosen and all the rest would obtain pardon.* This is precisely what Providence did not want. Able to do all, Providence disregards these pardons produced by impotence to punish. The great purification must be accomplished and eyes must be opened; the metal of France, freed from its sour and impure dross, must emerge cleaner and more malleable into the hands of a future king. Doubtless, Providence does not have to punish in this life in order to be justified, but in our epoch, coming down to our level, Providence punishes like a human tribunal.

There have been nations literally condemned to death like guilty individuals, and we know why.[15] If it entered

14. 'All eyes were turned away from so dreadful a sight. Such was the first and last punishment among the Romans of a kind that disregards the love of humanity.' Livy, I, 28, *de suppl. Mettii.* [Damiens, who made an unsuccessful attempt to assassinate Louis XV in 1757, was put to death in the manner prescribed for a regicide by being drawn and quartered. His execution lasted four hours.]

15. Leviticus 18:21–30; Deuteronomy 18:9–14; I Kings 15:24; IV Kings 17:7–18; 21:2; Herodotus, Bk. II, ch. 46, and Larcher's note on this passage.

into God's designs to reveal His plans with respect to the French Revolution, we would read the chastisement of the French like the decree of a parlement. But what more would we know? Is the chastisement not obvious? Have we not seen France dishonoured by more than a hundred thousand murders? The entire soil of this beautiful realm covered with scaffolds? And this unfortunate land watered with the blood of its children through judicial massacres, while inhuman tyrants squandered still more abroad for the support of a cruel war waged for their own interests? Never has a bloodier despot played with men's lives with such insolence, and never has a passive people presented themselves more complaisantly to the butcher. Sword and fire, cold and thirst, privations, sufferings of every kind— nothing slakes their taste for punishment; all who are assigned must play their parts, and no disobedience will be seen until the judgement is accomplished.[16]

And yet what interesting points to ponder in this cruel and disastrous war. We can pass by turns from sadness to admiration. Let us imagine ourselves at the most terrible moment of the Revolution. Suppose that under the government of the infernal committee the army by a sudden metamorphosis all at once became royalist. Suppose the army convoked its own primary assemblies and freely named its most enlightened and honourable men to trace out the route to be taken in this difficult situation. Finally, suppose that one of those elected by the army stood up and said,

16. [Maistre's manuscript continued, 'If this dreadful destruction of mankind and especially this mixture of the innocent falling with the guilty still frightens certain imaginations and appears to require explanation, one can try to say something; but one must nevertheless caution that there is no assured route for the man who immerses himself in the obscure paths of true metaphysics.']

'Brave and loyal warriors! There are circumstances where the sum total of human wisdom is reduced to choosing between different evils. Doubtless it is a hard thing to fight for the Committee of Public Safety. But to turn our arms against it would be even more fatal. The moment the army meddles in politics the state will be dissolved, and the enemies of France, profiting from this moment of dissolution, will invade and partition her. We must act, not for the present moment, but for the future; above all, we must maintain the integrity of France. All we can do is fight for the government, whatever it may be; for in this way, France, despite her internal discord, will preserve her military strength and her influence abroad. Taking things at their best, it is not for the government that we are fighting, but for France and the future king to whom we will deliver a greater empire, perhaps, than the Revolution found. So our duty is to overcome the repugnance that makes us hesitate. Perhaps our contemporaries will calumniate our conduct, but posterity will accord us justice.'

This man would have spoken like a great philosopher. Indeed, the army realized this chimerical hypothesis without knowing what it was doing. The terror on one side, immorality and extravagance on the other, have accomplished precisely what a consummate and almost prophetic wisdom would have ordered the army to do. When we think about it, we can see that once the revolutionary movement was established, only Jacobinism could have saved France and the monarchy.

The king has never had an ally, and although he was never so imprudent as to acknowledge the fact, it is evident enough that the coalition begrudged the integrity of France. So how was the coalition to be resisted? What supernatural means could confound the efforts of con-

spiring Europe? Only the infernal genius of Robespierre
could accomplish this prodigy. The revolutionary government hardened the soul of France by tempering it in
blood; the spirit of the soldiers was exasperated, and their
strength was doubled by ferocious despair and contempt
for life induced by rage. The horror of the scaffolds,
driving citizens to the frontiers, nourished external
force in the measure that the least internal resistance
was annihilated. All life, all wealth, all power was in
the hands of the revolutionary authority, and this monstrous power, drunk with blood and success, the most
frightful phenomenon that has ever been seen and the
like of which will never be seen again, was both a horrible
chastisement for the French and the sole means of saving
France.

What were the royalists asking for when they called for
their imagined counter-revolution, that is to say, one made
abruptly and by force? They requested, in fact, the conquest of France; they requested therefore her division, the
annihilation of her influence, and the debasement of her
king—which is to say, perhaps three centuries of massacres,
the inevitable consequence of such an upset of equilibrium.
But our descendants, who will worry very little about our
sufferings and will dance on our graves, will laugh at our
present ignorance; they will easily console themselves for
the excesses that we have seen and that will have preserved
the integrity of 'the most beautiful realm after that of
heaven'.[17]

All the monsters born of the Revolution have, apparently,
laboured only for the monarchy. Thanks to them, the lustre
of victories has won the admiration of the world and
surrounded the French name with a glory that the crimes

17. Grotius, *De Jure belli et pacis, Epist. ad Ludovicium XIII.*

of the Revolution can never entirely eclipse; thanks to them, the king will reascend his throne with all his pomp and power, perhaps even with an increase of power. And who knows whether, instead of miserably sacrificing some of his provinces to obtain the right to rule over the others, he might be restored with the pride of power that would enable him to give what he could withhold? Certainly less probable things have been seen to happen.

This same idea, that everything is happening for the advantage of the French monarchy, convinces me that any royalist revolution is impossible before peace is made, for the restoration of the throne would mean a sudden relaxation of the driving force of the state. The black magic working at the moment would disappear like mist before the sun. Kindness, clemency, justice, all the gentle and peaceful virtues, would suddenly reappear and would bring with them a general meekness of character, a certain cheerfulness entirely opposed to the sombre rigour of the revolutionary regime. No more requisitions, no more legalized thefts, no more violence. Would generals flying the white flag have condemned as *insurgents* the inhabitants of invaded countries who were merely defending themselves? And would these inhabitants have been ordered not to move under pain of being shot as rebels! These horrors, very useful to the future king, could not, however, be used by him. So he would have only humane means at his disposal. He would be on a par with his enemies, and what would happen in that moment of suspension that necessarily accompanies the transition from one regime to another? I do not know. I am quite aware that the great conquests of the French seem to put the integrity of the realm out of danger (I even believe I am touching here on the reason for these conquests). Nevertheless, it still appears more advantageous for France and the monarchy that the peace, and a glorious peace for the French, be made by the Republic, and that a profound peace protect the king from every kind of danger when he returns to the throne.[18]

On the other hand, it is apparent that violent revolution, far from curing the people, would confirm them in their errors and they would never forgive the power that snatched away their myths. Since the *people*, properly speaking, or the multitude, were needed by the rebels to overturn France, clearly they had, in general, to be spared, and the greatest burdens had to fall first on the wealthy class. So the weight of the usurping power must crush the people long enough to disgust them. They have only seen the Revolution; they must feel it; they must, so to speak, savour its bitter consequences. Perhaps, at the moment I am writing, they have not yet had enough.

A reaction must always be equal to the action. So do not be so impatient, and do not imagine that the very duration of your misfortunes promises you a *counter-revolution* of which you have no idea. Calm your resentment, and above all, complain not of kings and ask not for other miracles than those that you see. What! You contend that foreign powers are fighting disinterestedly to restore the French monarchy, and with no hope of indemnity? But then you do not expect men to be human; you ask the impossible. You will say, perhaps, that you would consent to the dismemberment of France for the *restoration of order*; but do you know what *order*? This is what will be seen in ten years—perhaps more, perhaps less. Who gives you the right to bargain for the king, for the French monarchy, and for your posterity? When blind rebels decree the indivisibility of the

18. [At the time Maistre was writing, in late 1796 or early 1797, France had made peace with Prussia and Spain, but was still at war with England and Austria.]

Republic, see only Providence decreeing that of the realm.[19]

Now let us take a look at the extraordinary persecution stirred up against the national religion and its ministers; this is one of the Revolution's most interesting *faces*.

No one would deny that the priesthood in France needed to be regenerated, and although I am far from adopting the popular declamations against the clergy, it appears to me that wealth, luxury, and a general inclination towards laxity had caused a decline of this great body, that the surplice often clothed a knight rather than an apostle, and that finally, in the period immediately preceding the Revolution, the clergy had gone down, nearly as much as the army, in the place it occupied in public opinion.

The first blow to the Church was the invasion of its properties,[20] the second was the constitutional oath,[21] and these two tyrannical measures began the regeneration. The oath sifted the clergy, if it may be put that way. All those who swore it, with some exceptions that may be disregarded, saw themselves led by degrees into an abyss of crime and disgrace; opinion is unanimous on these apostates.

The loyal priests, recommended to this same opinion by their initial act of firmness, rendered themselves even more illustrious by the intrepid way they braved sufferings and even death for the defence of their faith. The massacre of

19. [On 25 September 1792, the Convention declared that the French Republic was 'one and indivisible'.]

20. [The nationalization of the Church's property was voted by the Constituent Assembly on 16 April 1790. The legislation of 4 August 1789 had already abolished the tithe.]

21. [A decree of 27 November 1790 required all clerics holding ecclesiastical posts under the provisions of the Civil Constitution of the Clergy (12 July 1790) to take an oath to support the constitution. Most of the bishops and about half the parish priests refused; this was the beginning of a schism in the French church.]

the Carmelites compares in its nobility with anything in ecclesiastical history.[22]

The tyranny that, against all justice and decency, chased thousands of priests from their country was no doubt the most revolting imaginable; but here as before, the crimes of the French tyrants became the instruments of Providence. It was probably necessary that French priests be displayed to foreign nations; they have lived among Protestant peoples, and this coming together has greatly diminished hatreds and prejudices. The considerable emigration of clergy, especially French bishops, to England, appears to me a particularly remarkable event. Surely, words of peace will have been spoken and projects for reconciliation formed during this extraordinary meeting. Even if mutual hopes are all that result, this would be a lot. If ever Christians are to be reconciled, and everything suggests that they should, it seems that the initiative must come from the Church of England.[23] Presbyterianism was a French, and consequently an exaggerated, creation. We are too remote from the followers of this too-insubstantial religion; there are no means of getting to know one another. But the Anglican church, which touches us with one hand, touches with the other those whom we cannot approach. And although from one point of view, this church is exposed to attack from both sides and presents the slightly ridiculous spectacle of a

22. [During the September massacres (1792) some 116 priests were put to death at a Carmelite monastery in Paris.]

23. [Maistre was always interested in this possibility. In an unedited memoir on Freemasonry written in 1782, he had proposed achieving this goal by working quietly through the Masonic lodges. See *La Franc-Maçonnerie: Mémoire inédit au duc de Brunswick*, ed. E. Dermenghem (Paris: Rieder, 1925), pp. 97–104. In 1819, he hoped that Tsar Alexander would take up the task. See *Lettre à M. le Marquis sur l'état du Christianisme en Europe, Oeuvres*, 8: 515–16.]

rebel who preaches obedience, still from another point of view, it is very valuable and can perhaps be considered as one of those chemical intermediates capable of combining otherwise incompatible elements.

The property of the clergy having disappeared, everything conspires to restore the priesthood, since for a long time to come, new members are unlikely to be attracted by base motives. Moreover, there is reason to believe that contemplation of the work to be done will produce the kind of exaltation that raises men above themselves and makes them capable of accomplishing great things.

We must add to these circumstances the ferment of ideas in certain European countries, the exalted ideas of several remarkable men, and the kind of disquiet that is affecting religious dispositions, especially in Protestant lands, and is pushing some along extraordinary paths.[24]

At one and the same time we see the storm rumbling over Italy, Rome as well as Geneva menaced by the power that wants no religions,[25] and the national supremacy of religion in Holland abolished by a decree of the national convention.[26] If Providence *erases*, it is no doubt in order *to write.*

I also observe that when great creeds have established themselves in the world, they have been favoured by great

24. [Maistre had a life-long interest in Freemasonry, 'illuminism', and various currents of mysticism. This passage appears to refer to these movements. In the late 1790s in particular, a number of mystics, of whom Lavater and Klopstock were the most important, had considerable influence in Switzerland and Germany. See F. Baldensberger, *Le Mouvement des idées dans l'émigration française, 1789–1815* (Paris: Plan-Nourrit, 1925), 2: 185–217.]

25. [In early 1797, French armies were threatening both Geneva and Rome.]

26. [The National Assembly of the 'Batavian Republic' disestablished the Reformed church in 1796.]

conquests, by the formation of vast sovereignties, and the reason for this is apparent.

Finally, what is going to happen in our own time as a result of these extraordinary combinations that have deceived all human prudence? In truth, one would be tempted to believe that the political revolution is only a secondary object in the great plan unrolling before us with such terrible majesty.

I spoke, in the beginning, of the *magistracy* that France exercises over the rest of Europe. Providence, which always proportions the means to the end, and which gives to nations as to individuals the necessary organs for the accomplishment of their goals, has given the French nation precisely two instruments, two *arms*, so to speak, with which it stirs up the world—the French language and the spirit of proselytism that forms the essence of the nation's character. Consequently, France constantly has both the need and the power to influence men.

The power, I almost said the monarchy, of the French language is visible; you can at most only pretend to doubt it. And the spirit of proselytism is as obvious as the sun; from the fashion designer to the philosopher, it is the salient trait of the national character. This proselytism is commonly ridiculed, and really, in the forms it takes often merits ridicule. Fundamentally however, it is an *office*.

Moreover, there is an eternal law of the moral world that every *office* implies a duty. The Gallican church was a cornerstone of the Catholic system, or better, the Christian system, for in truth there is only the one. Although they may perhaps doubt it, churches opposing the universal Church subsist only by virtue of its existence, being similar to those parasitic plants, those sterile mistletoes that live only from the substance of the tree which supports them and which they impoverish.

Since the action and the reaction between opposing powers is always equal, it follows that the greatest efforts of the Goddess of Reason against Christianity should take place in France; the enemy attacked the citadel.

So the French clergy must remain alert; there are a thousand reasons for believing that they are being called to a great mission. And the same arguments that allow us to see why they have suffered also permit us to believe they are destined for a crucial task.

In a word, if there is no moral revolution in Europe, if the religious spirit is not reinforced in this part of the world, the social bond will dissolve. Nothing can be predicted, and anything must be expected, but if there is to be improvement in this matter, either France is called upon to produce it, or there is no analogy, no more induction, no more art of prediction.

This consideration especially makes me think that the French Revolution is a great epoch and that its consequences, in all kinds of ways, will be felt far beyond the time of its explosion and the limits of its birthplace.

Consideration of the political consequences of the Revolution confirms the same opinion. How the European powers have deceived themselves about France! How they have *meditated vain things*! Oh you who believe yourselves independent because you have no judges on this earth, never say, 'That suits me'; DISCITE JUSTITIAM MONITI![27] Whose hand was it that, severe and paternal at the same time, overwhelmed France with every imaginable calamity and sustained the empire with supernatural means by turning all the efforts of her enemies against themselves? Do not come and talk to us of *assignats*, the force of numbers, etc.,

27. ['Pay attention when the Lord punishes you.' Proverbs 3:11; Hebrews 12:5.]

for it is precisely the possibility of assignats and the force of numbers that is beyond nature. Moreover, neither paper money nor the advantage of numbers makes the winds favour French ships and repulse those of their enemies,[28] makes ice bridges the moment the French need them,[29] causes the sovereigns who oppose them to die at an appointed time,[30] allows the French to invade Italy without cannons,[31] or makes the reputedly bravest armies in the world throw down their arms to equal numbers and be taken prisoners.[32]

Read the fine reflections of M. Dumas on the present war;[33] *why* the war has taken its present character is perfectly clear, but the *how* is not. We must always go back to the Committee of Public Safety, which performed a miracle and whose spirit is still winning battles.

In summary, the chastisement of the *French*, as well as the protection accorded to France, departs from all the ordinary rules. But these two miracles together multiply each other and present one of the most astonishing spectacles that humanity has ever seen.

28. [In June 1794, thirty-eight English ships failed to prevent a French grain convoy escorted by only three French frigates from reaching France.]

29. [In 1795, in Holland, a French cavalry unit captured an English fleet trapped in the ice.]

30. [The Swedish king, Gustavus III, was assassinated in March 1792, just when he was about to march against France. Catherine the Great of Russia, a determined opponent of the French Revolution, died in November 1796.]

31. [Napoleon in his first Italian campaign in April 1796 was short of artillery because of a lack of horses to move his cannon.]

32. [Probably a reference to Napoleon's rapid victories over the Piedmontese in April 1796, which from Maistre's Piedmontese point of view, seemed inexplicable.]

33. [Mathieu Dumas, an émigré French officer, published a book entitled *Des Résultats de la dernière campagne* in 1797.]

As events unfold, more answers and more wondrous relationships will be seen. Moreover, I see only a portion of the things that a more penetrating view could have discovered at the present time. The horrible effusion of human blood occasioned by this great upheaval is a terrible means; nevertheless, it is a means as much as a punishment, and it can be the subject of interesting reflections.

III

On the Violent Destruction of the Human Species

The king of Dahomey, in the African interior, was not so wrong, unfortunately, when he recently told an Englishman, 'God made the world for war; all realms, great and small, have always practised it, although on different principles.'[1]

Unhappily, history proves that war is, in a certain sense, the habitual state of mankind, which is to say that human blood must flow without interruption somewhere or other on the globe, and that for every nation, peace is only a respite.

The closing of the temple of Janus under Augustus can be cited;[2] there was one year in Charlemagne's warlike

1. *The History of Dahomey* by Archibald Dalzel, Biblioth. Brit., May 1796, Vol. 2, no. 1, p. 87.

2. [It was a Roman custom that the doors of the temple of Janus were kept open in time of war and locked in time of peace. Up through the time of Augustus, these doors were closed only four times, twice during his reign.]

reign (the year of 790) when there was no war.[3] One can point to a short period after the Peace of Ryswick in 1697 and another equally short after that of Carlowitz in 1699 when there was no war, not only in Europe, but even in all the known world. But these are merely exceptions. Moreover, who can know what is happening over the entire globe at a given time?

The century that is just ending began, for France, with a cruel war that was not terminated until the Treaty of Rastadt in 1714. In 1719, France declared war on Spain; the Treaty of Paris put an end to it in 1727.[4] The election of the king of Poland rekindled war in 1733; the peace was made in 1736. Four years later, the terrible War of the Austrian Succession broke out and lasted without interruption until 1748. Peace was beginning to heal up the wounds of eight years of war when, eight years later, the ambition of England forced France to take up arms again. The Seven Years' War is too well known. After fifteen years of peace, the American Revolution involved France anew in a war the consequences of which all human wisdom could not foresee.[5] The peace was signed in 1782; seven years later the Revolution began. It still continues, and it has cost France perhaps three million men so far.[6]

Thus, considering France alone, here are forty years of

3. *Histoire de Charlemagne*, by M. Gaillard, Vol. II, Bk. I, ch. v.

4. [Peace was signed between France and Spain in Madrid in 1720. The Treaty of Paris of 1727 was only a convention by which Spain and England (still at war) accepted French arbitration.]

5. [Maistre evidently regarded French involvement in the American War of Independence as one of the causes of the French Revolution.]

6. [The figure of three million is exaggerated.]

war out of ninety-six. If there are nations more fortunate, there are also many less fortunate.

But it is not enough to consider one period of time and one spot on the globe; one must look at the long series of massacres that has soiled every page of history. One sees war raging without interruption, like a continuing fever marked by terrifying paroxysms. I ask the reader to follow the record since the decline of the Roman republic.

In one battle Marius exterminated two hundred thousand Cimbri and Teutons.[7] Mithridates slaughtered eighty thousand Romans.[8] Sulla killed ninety thousand men in a battle fought in Boeotia, where he lost ten thousand himself.[9] Soon you see civil wars and proscriptions. Caesar alone killed a million men on the battlefield (before him, Alexander had had this melancholy honour). Augustus closed the temple of Janus momentarily, but he reopened it for centuries by establishing an elective empire. A few good princes gave the state a breathing spell, but war never ceased, and under the rule of the *good* Titus, six hundred thousand men perished in the siege of Jerusalem.[10] The destruction of men brought about by the Roman armies is truly frightening.[11] The late empire is nothing but a series of massacres. To begin with Constantine, what wars and what battles! Licinius loses twenty thousand men at Cibalis, thirty-four thousand at Adrianople, and a hundred

7. [Marius, a famous Roman general, defeated these barbarian tribes at Vercelli in Italy in 101 B.C.]

8. [Mithridates VI Eupator (120–63 B.C.), king of Pontus, conquered parts of Asia Minor and bitterly opposed Roman expansion in this area before he was finally defeated by Pompey.]

9. [Sulla (138–78 B.C.) was another Roman general.]

10. [The siege of Jerusalem occurred in A.D. 70.]

11. Montesquieu, *Esprit des lois*, Bk. XXIII, ch. xix.

thousand at Chrysoupolis.[12] The Nordic peoples begin to move. The Franks, the Goths, the Huns, the Lombards, the Alans, the Vandals, etc. attack the empire and successively tear it to pieces. Attila puts Europe to fire and sword. The Franks kill more than two hundred thousand of his men near Châlons,[13] and the Goths, the following year, cost him more still. In less than a century, Rome was taken and sacked three times; and in a revolt that broke out in Constantinople, forty thousand people were slaughtered. The Goths made themselves masters of Milan and killed three hundred thousand inhabitants. Totila massacred all the inhabitants of Tivoli and ninety thousand men at the sack of Rome.[14]

Mohammed appears; the sword and Koran overrun two-thirds of the world. The Saracens sail from the Euphrates to the Guadalquivir. The immense city of Syracuse is razed to its foundations; they lose thirty thousand men in a single naval combat near Constantinople, and Pelagius kills twenty thousand of them in a land battle.[15] These losses were nothing for the Saracens; but the torrent encountered the genius of the Franks on the plain of Tours, where the son of the first Pepin, in the midst of three hundred thousand cadavers, attached to his name the terrible epithet that distinguishes it still.[16]

Islam is carried to Spain and finds there an indomitable

12. [Valerius Licinius, Constantine's brother-in-law, shared power with him (313–23) until attacked by Constantine. He was defeated in the battles named by Maistre.]

13. [The battle of Châlons took place in 451.]

14. [Totila was king of the Ostrogoths in Italy (541–52).]

15. [Pelagius (718–37) was the first Christian king of Spain during the Moorish period.]

16. [Charles Martel (*martel* means 'hammer') defeated the Saracens at the battle of Tours (732). The casualties were certainly much lower than Maistre suggests.]

rival.[17] Perhaps never has more glory, more grandeur, and more carnage been seen than in the eight-hundred-year struggle between Christians and Muslims in Spain. Several expeditions, several battles even, cost twenty, thirty, forty, up to eighty thousand lives.

Charlemagne ascends the throne, and there is a half-century of fighting. Every year he decrees death for some portion of Europe. Active everywhere and everywhere the conqueror, he wipes out iron-strong nations as easily as Caesar wiped out the effeminate men of Asia. The Normans begin that long series of ravages and cruelties that still make us shudder. Charlemagne's immense heritage is torn apart; ambition covers it with blood, and the name of the Franks disappears at the battle of Fontenay.[18] All Italy is pillaged by the Saracens while the Normans, Danes, and Hungarians ravage France, Holland, England, Germany, and Greece. The barbarian nations are finally established and tamed. This vein yields no more blood; another is opened immediately with the beginning of the Crusades. All Europe throws itself on Asia; the number of victims can be counted only in myriads. Genghis Khan and his sons subjugate and ravage the world from China to Bohemia. The French, who are involved in crusades against the Muslims, also crusade against the heretics in the cruel Albigensian war.[19] In the battle of Bouvines, thirty thousand men lose their lives.[20] Five years later, eighty thousand

17. [Catholicism.]

18. [The battle of Fontenay (841) saw the defeat of Lothair, Charlemagne's successor as emperor, by his brothers, Louis the German and Charles the Bald.]

19. [The Albigensian Crusade (1209–29) was a campaign against the Albigensian heretics in southern France.]

20. [Otto IV, the Holy Roman emperor, was defeated at Bouvines in 1214 by Philip Augustus of France.]

Saracens perish at the siege of Damietta.[21] Guelphs and Ghibellines begin the conflict that will stain Italy with blood for so long.[22] The torch of civil war is kindled in Germany. Then the Sicilian Vespers.[23] Under the reigns of Edward and Philip of Valois, France and England hurl themselves at each other more violently than ever and create a new era of carnage. The massacre of Jews. The battle of Poitiers.[24] The battle of Nicopolis.[25] The vanquisher falls under the blows of Tamerlane, who repeats Genghis Khan. The duke of Burgundy has the duke of Orléans assassinated, and the bloody rivalry of these two families begins.[26] The battle of Agincourt.[27] The Hussites put much of Germany to fire and sword. Mohammed II reigns and fights for thirty years.[28] England, forced back within its own frontiers, is torn apart by internal troubles as the houses

21. [Damietta, in Egypt, was besieged by Saint Louis in 1249 during the Seventh Crusade.]

22. [The Guelphs, the papal party, and the Ghibellines, the imperial party, were engaged in bitter rivalry from the thirteenth through the fifteenth centuries.]

23. [The Sicilian Vespers was an uprising against the Angevin monarchy in Sicily which began on Easter Sunday, 1282.]

24. [Poitiers (1356) was a French defeat at the hands of Edward, the Black Prince.]

25. [Nicopolis was a city on the Danube where a 'crusading' expedition under King Sigismund of Hungary was defeated by the Turks in 1396.]

26. [The assassination of the duke of Orléans in 1407 was followed by a civil war between the Armagnacs (from the duke of Orléan's father-in-law, the count of Armagnac) and the Burgundians.]

27. [Agincourt (1415) was another English victory over the French.]

28. [Mohammed II, the Conqueror, who reigned from 1451 to 1481, brought the Byzantine Empire to an end by his conquest of Constantinople in 1453.]

of York and Lancaster bathe the country in blood.[29] The Burgundian heiress joins her states to the house of Austria, and in this marriage contract it is written that men will slaughter each other for centuries from the Baltic to the Mediterranean.[30] The discovery of the new world means the death sentence for three million Indians. Charles V and Francis I appear on the world stage, and every page of their history is red with human blood. The reign of Suleiman.[31] The battle of Mohacs.[32] The siege of Vienna,[33] the siege of Malta,[34] etc. But it is from the shadow of a cloister that there emerges one of mankind's very greatest scourges. Luther appears; Calvin follows him. The Peasants' Revolt; the Thirty Years' War; the civil war in France; the massacre of the Low Countries; the massacre of Ireland; the massacre of the Cévennes; St. Bartholomew's Day; the murders of Henry II, Henry IV, Mary Stuart, and Charles I; and finally, in our day, from the same source, the French Revolution.[35]

I will not carry this frightful catalogue any further; our own century and the preceding one are too well known. If you go back to the birth of nations, if you come down to our own day, if you examine peoples in all possible conditions from the state of barbarism to the most advanced civilization, you always find war. From this primary cause, and

29. [The Wars of the Roses (1455–85).]

30. [The marriage of the heiress of the duke of Burgundy to Maximilian of Austria was a first step in the creation of the dynastic empire of their grandson, Charles V, and the Hapsburg-Valois rivalry.]

31. [Suleiman the Magnificent, Sultan of Turkey (1520–66).]

32. [Defeat of the Hungarians by the Turks in 1526.]

33. [The first siege of Vienna by the Turks in 1529.]

34. [Malta was besieged by the Turks in 1565.]

35. [Maistre blamed all these events, including the French Revolution, on Protestantism. See his 'Réflexions sur le protestantisme dans ses rapports avec la souveraineté', Oeuvres, 8: 63–97.]

from all the other connected causes, the effusion of human blood has never ceased in the world. Sometimes blood flows less abundantly over some larger area, sometimes it flows more abundantly in a more restricted area, but the flow remains nearly constant.

But from time to time the flow is augmented prodigiously by such extraordinary events as the Punic Wars, the Triumvirate, the victories of Caesar, the irruption of the barbarians, the Crusades, the wars of religion, the Spanish Succession, the French Revolution, etc. If one had a table of massacres similar to a meteorological table, who knows whether, after centuries of observation, some law might not be discovered?[36] Buffon has proven quite clearly that a large percentage of animals are destined to die a violent death.[37] He could apparently have extended the demonstration to man; but let the facts speak for themselves.

Yet there is room to doubt whether this violent destruction is, in general, such a great evil as is believed; at least, it is one of those evils that enters into an order of things where everything is violent and *against nature*, and that produces compensations. First, when the human soul has lost its strength through laziness, incredulity, and the gangrenous vices that follow an excess of civilization, it can be retempered only in blood. Certainly there is no easy

36. There is, for example, the report made by the chief surgeon of the Imperial Army that 33,543 of the 215,000 men employed by the Emperor Joseph II against the Turks from 1 June 1788 to 1 May 1789 perished from illness, while 80,000 were killed in action. And according to an approximate calculation made in Germany, up to October 1795, the present war has already cost France a million men and the allies 500,000. 'Extrait d'un ouvrage periodique Allemand' in the *Courrier de Francfort*, 28 October 1795, no. 296.

37. [Buffon (1707–88) was a famous French naturalist, some of whose speculations anticipated Darwin.]

explanation of why war produces different effects in different circumstances. But it can be seen clearly enough that mankind may be considered as a tree which an invisible hand is continually pruning and which often profits from the operation. In truth the tree may perish if the trunk is cut or if the tree is overpruned; but who knows the limits of the human tree? What we do know is that excessive carnage is often allied with excessive population, as was seen especially in the ancient Greek republics and in Spain under the Arab domination.[38] Platitudes about war mean nothing. One need not be very clever to know that when more men are killed, fewer remain at the moment, just as it is true that the more branches one cuts off, the fewer remain on the tree. But the results of the operation are what must be considered. Moreover, following the same comparison, we may observe that the skilful gardener directs the pruning less towards lush vegetation than towards the fructification of the tree; he wants fruit, not wood or leaves. Now the real fruits of human nature—the arts, sciences, great enterprises, lofty conceptions, manly virtues—are due especially to the state of war. We know that nations have never achieved the highest point of the greatness of which they are capable except after long and bloody wars. Thus, Greece's most brilliant hour was the terrible epoch of the Peloponnesian War; the Age of Augustus followed immediately the civil war and the proscriptions; French genius was hewn by the League and polished by the Fronde; all the great men of the century of Queen Anne

38. Spain at that time had something like forty million inhabitants; today it has only ten. 'In the old days, Greece flourished in the midst of cruel wars; blood flowed in torrents, but the land was thickly peopled. *It seemed,* said Machiavelli, *that in spite of murder, proscription, and civil strife, our republic became stronger than ever, etc.*' Rousseau, *Contrat social,* Bk. III, ch. x.

were born in the midst of political upheavals. In a word, we can say that blood is the manure of the plant we call *genius*.

I wonder if those who say that *the arts are the friends of peace* really know what they are saying. It would at least be necessary to explain and circumscribe the proposition, for I see nothing less pacific than the centuries of Alexander and Pericles, of Augustus, of Leo X and Francis I, of Louis XIV and Queen Anne.

Could the shedding of human blood possibly not have serious causes and serious effects? Let us reflect; history and fable, the discoveries of modern physiology and antique tradition all unite to furnish material for these meditations. We should not be more ashamed of speculating on this subject than on a thousand others less relevant to man.

In the meantime let us thunder against war and try to teach sovereigns an aversion to it; but let us not give in to the dreams of Condorcet, that *philosophe* so dear to the Revolution who used his life to prepare the unhappiness of the present generation, graciously willing perfection to posterity.[39] There is only one way of restraining the scourge of war, and that is by restraining the disorders that lead to this terrible purification.

In the Greek tragedy of Orestes, Helen, one of the characters in the play, is taken away by the gods to the just resentment of the Greeks, and placed in the sky beside her two brothers to be a guiding sign to navigators. Apollo appears in order to justify this strange apotheosis.[40] 'Helen's beauty', he says, 'was only an instrument that the gods used

39. [Condorcet, whose famous *Esquisse d'un tableau historique des progrès de l'esprit humain* (1794) was written while he was in hiding during the Terror, seemed to Maistre the worst example of a blind optimist.]

40. 'A point worthy of him who maintains it.' Horace, *Ars Poetica*, 191.

to set the Greeks and Trojans against each other to cause their blood to flow, in order to quench on earth the iniquity of men become too numerous.'[41]

Apollo spoke very well. Men gather the clouds, and then they complain of the tempests that follow. 'It is the anger of kings that arms the earth; it is the anger of heaven that arms the kings.'[42]

I know well that in all these considerations we are continually troubled by the wearisome sight of the innocent who perish with the guilty. But without becoming deeply involved in this most profound question, we can consider it solely in the light of the age-old dogma that *the innocent suffer for the benefit of the guilty.*

It was from this dogma, it seems to me, that the ancients derived the custom of sacrifices that was practised everywhere and that was judged useful not only for the living but also for the dead,[43] a typical custom that habit has led us to regard without astonishment, but whose roots are nonetheless difficult to discover.

Self-sacrifices, so famous in antiquity, come from the same dogma. Decius[44] had *faith* that the sacrifice of his life would be accepted by the Divinity and that he could use it to balance all the evils that menaced his country.[45]

41. Euripides, *Orestes*, 1655–58.

42. [The verse is by J.-B. Rousseau.]

43. They sacrificed, literally, 'for the repose of souls; and these sacrifices', Plato says, 'are of great efficacity, as has been said by entire cities, by poets born of the gods, and by prophets inspired by the gods'. Plato, *De Republica*, Bk. II.

44. [Decius was the name of three Romans who are supposed to have sacrificed themselves to the gods to secure victories for the Roman armies in 340, 295, and 290 B.C.]

45. 'To expiate all anger of the gods . . . the one had drawn all the threats and menaces of the supernal and infernal gods upon himself alone.' Livy, VIII, 9 and 10.

Christianity came to consecrate this dogma, which is perfectly natural to man although appearing difficult to arrive at by reason.

Thus, there could have been in the heart of Louis XVI, in that of the saintly Elizabeth,[46] such an impulse, such an acceptance, capable of saving France.

Sometimes it is asked, Of what use are these terrible austerities, which are also self-sacrifices, practised by certain religious orders? It would be precisely the same thing to ask of what use is Christianity, which rests entirely on an enlargement of this same dogma of innocence paying for crime.[47]

The authority that approves these orders chooses certain men and *insulates* them from the world in order to make them *conductors*.

There is nothing but violence in the universe; but we are spoiled by a modern philosophy that tells us *all is good*,[48] whereas evil has tainted everything, and in a very real sense, *all is evil*, since nothing is in its place. The keynote of the system of our creation has been lowered, and following the rules of harmony, all the others have been lowered proportionately. *All creation groans*,[49] and tends with pain and effort towards another order of things.

46. [Madame Elizabeth, who was executed in 1794, was a younger sister of Louis XVI.]

47. [Maistre develops this theme in his *Eclaircissement sur les sacrifices, Oeuvres*, 5: 283–360.]

48. [*Tout est bien.* Maistre is castigating the 'best of all possible worlds' optimism that seemed to characterize some eighteenth-century thinkers. Of course Maistre was not alone in this reaction; Voltaire's *Candide*, for example, included a brilliant satire on philosophical optimism.]

49. St. Paul to the Romans, 8:22. Charles Bonnet's system of Palingenesis has some similarities with St. Paul's text; but this idea does not take him to that of a prior degradation. Neverthe-

The spectators of great human calamities, especially, are led to these sad meditations. But let us not lose courage: there is no chastisement that does not purify; there is no disorder that ETERNAL LOVE does not turn against the principle of evil. It is gratifying amid the general upheaval to have a presentiment of the plans of Divinity. We will never see the complete picture during our earthly sojourn, and often we will deceive ourselves; but in all possible sciences, except the exact sciences, are we not reduced to conjecture? And if our conjectures are plausible, if there are analogies for them, if they are based on universally accepted ideas, above all if they are consoling and suited to make us better men, what do they lack? If they are not true, they are good; or rather, since they are good, are they not true?

Having envisaged the French Revolution from a purely moral point of view, I now turn my speculations to politics, without, however, forgetting the primary aim of my work.

---

less they agree quite well. [Charles Bonnet (1720–93) was a Swiss naturalist and philosopher whose philosophical theories combined Leibnizian and Christian metaphysics. His *Palingénésie philosophique* was published in 1769.]

IV

Can the French
Republic Last?

It would be better to ask whether the Republic can exist.[1] The assumption is made, but too hastily, and the *preliminary* question seems quite justified, for nature and history together prove that a large indivisible republic is an impossibility. A small number of republicans closed up within the walls of a city can undoubtedly have millions of subjects; this was the case with Rome. But a large and free nation cannot exist under a republican government. The thing is so clear in itself that theory could dispense with experience; but here experience, which decides every question in politics as in physics, is perfectly in accord with theory.

What could have been said to the French to get them to believe in a republic of twenty-four million people? Two things only: (1) nothing prevents us from doing something

1. [This chapter is apparently a direct response to Benjamin Constant's 'Objections Drawn from Experience against the Possibility of a Republic in a Large State'. See his *De la Force du gouvernement actuel et de la nécessité de s'y rallier* (Paris: 1796). Constant argued from the possibility of progress.]

that has never been seen before; (2) the discovery of the representative system makes possible for us what was impossible for our predecessors. Let us examine the strength of these two arguments.

If we are told that a die thrown a billion times had never turned up anything but five numbers—1, 2, 3, 4, and 5— could we believe that there was a 6 on one of the faces? NO, undoubtedly; and it would be as obvious to us as if we had seen it that one of the faces is blank or that one of the numbers is repeated.

Well then! Let us run through history; there you will see so-called Fortune tirelessly throwing the die for over four thousand years. Has LARGE REPUBLIC ever been rolled? No. Therefore, that number is not on the die.

If the world had seen the successive development of new forms of government, we would have no right to affirm that such-and-such a form of government is impossible because it has never been seen. But things are exactly the opposite; monarchies have always existed, and sometimes republics. If we want to go into the subdivisions, we can call government where the masses exercise sovereignty *democracy*, and that where sovereignty belongs to a more or less restricted number of privileged families *aristocracy*. And everything has been said.

The comparison with the die is perfectly exact; the same numbers always coming from the horn of Fortune, we are authorized by the theory of probabilities to affirm that there are no others.

Let us not confuse the essences of things with their modifications: the first are unalterable and always remain the same, the second change and vary the spectacle a little, at least for the multitude; but every experienced eye will easily penetrate the changing cloak with which eternal nature is enveloped according to time and place.

For example, what is peculiar and new about the three powers that constitute the government of England? The names of the *Peers* and the *Commons*, the costumes of the lords, etc. But the three powers, considered in the abstract, are to be found wherever a wise and lasting liberty is to be found; above all, they were found in Sparta, where the government, before Lycurgus, 'was always in oscillation, inclining at one time to tyranny when the kings had too much power and at another time to popular confusion when the common people had usurped too much authority'. But Lycurgus placed the senate between the two, so that it was, according to Plato, 'a salutary counterweight ... and a strong barrier holding the two extremities in equal balance and giving a firm and assured foundation to the health of the state, because the senators ... ranged themselves on the side of the king when there was need to resist popular temerity, and on the other hand, just as strongly took the part of the people against the king to prevent the latter from usurping a tyrannical power'.[2]

Thus, nothing is new, and a large republic is impossible, since there has never been a large republic.

As for the representative system, which some people believe capable of resolving the problem, I hope I will be pardoned for a digression.

Let us begin by noting that this system is by no means a modern discovery, but was a *production*, or better, a *piece*, of feudal government when the latter attained that state of maturity and equilibrium which made it, all things considered, the most perfect in the world.[3]

Having formed the communes, the royal authority called

2. Plutarch, *Life of Lycurgus*, Amyot's translation.
3. 'I do not believe that there has ever been such a well-tempered government on the earth.' Montesquieu, *Esprit des lois*, Bk. XI, ch. viii.

them to the national assemblies; they could appear there only through their mandatories, and this is how the representative system began.

In passing, the same thing may be said of trial by jury. Within the hierarchy of tenures the vassals of the same order were called to the courts of their respective suzerains; from this was born the maxim that every man must be judged by his peers (*Pares curtis*).[4] The English have maintained the idea in its full extent and have even developed it from its original sense; but the French, less tenacious, or ceding perhaps to invincible circumstances, have not extended it to the same degree.

One would have to be incapable of penetrating to what Bacon calls the *interiora rerum* to imagine that men could have erected such institutions by anterior reasoning or that they could be the fruit of deliberation.

Moreover, national representation is not peculiar to England: it is to be found in every European monarchy; although it is alive in Great Britain, elsewhere it is dead or sleeping. To consider if its suspension is humanity's misfortune or if we should return to the old forms is beyond the scope of this little work. Let the following historical observations suffice: (1) in England, where national representation has gained and retained more strength than anywhere else, there is no mention of such a thing before the thirteenth century;[5] (2) the system was not an invention, or the result of deliberation, or the result of the action of the people making use of their ancient rights, but was, in

4. See the *Book of Fiefs*, following Roman Law.
5. English democrats have tried to push the origins of the rights of the Commons much further back and have even found them in the famous witenagemots; but they have had to abandon with good grace this untenable thesis. Hume, Vol. I, Appendix I,

reality, the work of an ambitious soldier, who, after the battle of Lewes, created the balance of the three powers without knowing what he was doing, as always happens;[6] (3) not only was the convocation of the Commons to the National Council a concession of the monarch, but in the beginning the king named the representatives of the provinces, cities, and boroughs; (4) even after the Commons arrogated to themselves the right of sending representatives to Parliament during Edward I's journey to Palestine, they had there only a consultative voice; they presented their *grievances*, like the Estates-General in France, and the formula for the concessions emanating from the throne as a result of their petitions was always *Granted by the King and the spiritual and temporal lords on the humble prayers of the Commons*; and finally, (5) the attribution of co-legislative power to the House of Commons is still quite new, since it scarcely goes back to the middle of the fifteenth century.

So if the phrase 'national representation' is understood to mean a *certain* number of representatives sent by *certain* men taken from *certain* cities and boroughs by virtue of an old concession by the sovereign, there is no dispute—such a government exists, and it is that of England. But if the phrase is understood to mean that *all* the people are represented, that they may be represented

---

p. 144; Appendix II, p. 407 (London, 1762). [The witenagemot, or witan, was the council of 'wise men' upon whom the Anglo-Saxon kings could call for advice.]

6. [The battle of Lewes (1264) was a victory for the barons, led by Simon de Montfort, over King Henry III. The next year, for the first time, burgesses elected by the boroughs were summoned to Parliament along with prelates, barons, and knights. The relationship between these events was not as clear-cut as Maistre suggests.]

only by virtue of a mandate,[7] and that every citizen, with some physically and morally inevitable exceptions, is able to give or receive these mandates, and if there is also a claim to join to such an order of things the abolition of all hereditary distinctions and offices, this representation is a thing that has never been seen and that will never succeed.[8]

America is often cited. I know of nothing so provoking as the praises bestowed on this babe-in-arms. Let it grow.

But to make this discussion as clear as possible, we must note that the instigators of the French republic are bound to prove not only that *perfected* representation (so styled by the innovators) is possible and good, but also that the people can by this means retain their sovereignty (again, so they say) and form, in their totality, a republic. This is the crux of the question, for if the *republic* is in the capital and the rest of France is *subject* to the republic, the republic is not accountable to the *sovereign people*.

The recent commission that was charged with proposing a method of national representation estimated the French population at thirty million. Let us accept this number and assume that France keeps her conquests. Each year, according to the terms of the constitution, two hundred and fifty members of the legislative body will be replaced by two hundred and fifty others. So if the assumed fifteen

7. It is often assumed, either through bad faith or inattention, that only a mandatory can be a representative. This is an error. Children, fools, and absentees are represented every day in the courts by men who hold their mandate from the law only; moreover, the *people* eminently combine these three characteristics, for they are always *childish*, always *foolish*, and always *absent*. So why should their *tutors* not dispense with their mandates?

8. [The Constitution of the Year III declared, 'Equality does not admit of any distinction of birth or any inheritance of powers.']

million males in the population were immortal, qualified as representatives, and named in rotation, then each Frenchman would exercise his turn at national sovereignty once in every sixteen thousand years. But since some men cannot be prevented from dying from time to time in this interval, and since moreover, some people may be elected more than once, and since many individuals, by nature and good sense, will always be ineligible as national representatives, the imagination is staggered by the prodigious number of sovereigns condemned to die without having reigned.[9]

Rousseau maintained that *the national will cannot be delegated*; one may agree or not and debate such academic questions a thousand years, but what is sure is that the representative system directly excludes the exercise of sovereignty, especially in the French system, where the rights of the people are limited to selecting electors and where not only are the people unable to give special mandates to their representatives, but the law carefully severs all relations between representatives and their respective provinces by warning them that *they are not sent by those who sent them*, but by the *nation*,[10] a wonderfully convenient word, since one makes of it whatever one wishes. In short, it is impossible to imagine a system better calculated to annihilate the rights of the people.

Thus that vile Jacobin conspirator was quite right when he declared roundly during a judicial inquiry, 'I believe the present government a usurper of authority, a violator of all the rights of the people, who have been reduced to the most deplorable slavery. It is a frightful system of the happiness

9. I am not counting the five places as Directors. For these, the chance is so small that it can be considered zero.

10. [Article 52 of the Constitution of 1795 states, 'The members of the Legislative Body are not representatives of the department which has elected them, but of the entire nation.']

of the few founded on the oppression of the masses. The people are so muzzled, so loaded with chains by this aristocratic government, that it is becoming more difficult than ever for them to break them.'[11]

So what does this vain honour of representation mean to the nation when it is involved so indirectly and when millions of individuals will never participate? Are sovereignty and government any less alien to them?

But, they say in answering the argument, what does it matter to the nation whether representation is a vain honour, if the system establishes public liberty?

This is not the question. The question is not whether the French people can be *free* with the constitution they have been given, but whether they can be *sovereign*. They change the question to escape the logic. Let us begin by excluding the exercise of sovereignty and insist on the fundamental point that the sovereign will always be in Paris, that all this noise about representation means nothing, that the *people* remain perfectly alien to government, that they are more subject than they were under a monarchy, and that the phrase *large republic*, like *square circle*, is self-contradictory. Moreover, the argument has been demonstrated arithmetically.

The question may be reduced to finding out whether the interests of the French people are served by being *subject* to an executive directory and two councils as instituted by the 1795 constitution rather than to a king reigning

11. See the interrogation of Babeuf, June 1796. ['Gracchus' Babeuf has an honoured position in the history of socialism, but he might be characterized more accurately as a primitive communist who combined the traditional demand for the abolition of poverty with a willingness to use terror and a Jacobin style of dictatorship to achieve his ideal. His Conspiracy of the Equals against the Directory failed miserably, and he was executed in May 1797.]

according to the old forms. There is much less difficulty in resolving a problem than in posing it.

So we must discard this word *republic* and speak only of the government. I will not discuss whether or not this government is fit to secure the public welfare; the French know the answer well enough! But given its nature, no matter what it is called, let us see if one may believe in its permanence.

Let us first of all raise ourselves to a level that befits an intelligent being, and from this elevated point of view, consider the origins of this government.

Evil has nothing in common with life; it cannot create, since its power is purely negative. *Evil is the schism of being; it is not true.*

Now what distinguishes the French Revolution and makes it an *event* unique in history is that it is radically *bad*. No element of good disturbs the eye of the observer; it is the highest degree of corruption ever known; it is pure impurity.

On what page of history will you find such a great quantity of vices assembled at one time on the same stage? What a horrible assemblage of baseness and cruelty! What profound immorality! What absence of all decency!

The characteristics of the springtime of liberty are so striking that it is impossible to be mistaken. It is a time when love of the fatherland is a religion and respect for the laws a superstition, a time of sturdy character and austere morals, when every virtue flourishes at once, when factions benefit the fatherland because they fight only for the honour of serving it, when everything, even crime, carries the mark of greatness.

If this picture is compared to the one offered us by France, how can anyone believe in the permanence of a liberty that springs from gangrene? Or, more precisely, how can one believe that this liberty can be born (since it does not as yet exist) or that from the heart of the most disgusting corruption there can emerge the form of government that less than any other may dispense with virtue? When one hears these so-called republicans talk of liberty and virtue, one thinks of a faded courtesan with rouged blushes putting on the airs of a virgin.

A republican journal reports the following anecdote on Parisian morals today: 'A case of seduction was pleaded before the Civil Tribunal. A young girl of fourteen astonished the judges by a degree of corruption that more than matched the profound immorality of her seducer. More than half the audience was composed of young women and young girls; among them more than twenty were no more than thirteen or fourteen, several being with their mothers. And instead of covering their faces, they laughed loudly at the necessary but disgusting details that made the men blush.'[12]

I ask the reader to recall that Roman citizen who, in the days of Roman greatness, was punished for having embraced his wife before his children. Draw the parallel and your own conclusion.[13]

No doubt the French Revolution has lasted long enough to go through several phases; nevertheless, its general character has never varied, and from its birth there was evidence of what it would become. There was a certain inexplicable delirium, a blind impetuosity, a scandalous contempt for everything respectable, a new kind of atrocity that joked about its crimes, and especially, an impudent prostitution of reasoning and of every word meant to express ideas of justice and virtue.

12. *Journal de l'opposition*, 1795, no. 175, p. 705.
13. [According to Plutarch, Cato the Elder, as censor, expelled Manilius from the Senate for having embraced his wife in front of his daughter.]

In particular, if we consider the acts of the National Assembly, it is difficult to find anything to approve. When I think back to the time of its meeting, I sense myself transported like the sublime bard of England to an imaginary world; I see mankind's enemy seated in the Riding School and calling every *evil spirit* to this new *pandemonium*;[14] I hear distinctly *il rauco suon delle tartare trombe*,[15] and I see all the vices of France hasten to the call. And I am not so sure that all this is an allegory.

And notice again how crime forms the foundation of the entire republican edifice: this word 'citizen', which they have substituted for the old forms of courtesy, is addressed to the vilest of humans; the brigands invented this new title in one of their legislative orgies.[16] The republican calendar, which must not be seen merely as something ridiculous, was a conspiracy against religion. Their era dates from the greatest crimes that have ever dishonoured humanity; they cannot date an act without covering themselves with shame and recalling the dishonourable origin of a government whose very holidays are frightening.

So can a durable government emerge from this bloody mire? To be sure the savage and licentious morals of barbarian peoples have not prevented their eventual civilization; barbarous ignorance has no doubt presided over the establishment of a number of political systems, but learned barbarism, systematic atrocity, calculated corruption, and, above all, irreligion have never produced any-

14. [The capital of hell in Milton's *Paradise Lost* was called Pandemonium.]

15. ['The raucous sound of infernal trumpets'. Tasso, *Jerusalem Delivered*, Chant IV, 3.]

16. [The famous Declaration of Rights of Man and the Citizen was voted 19 August 1789.]

thing. Greenness leads to maturity; rottenness leads to nothing.

Moreover, who has ever seen a government, and in particular a free constitution, originate despite its members and without their consent?[17] But this is the phenomenon that would be presented to us if this meteor called the *French Republic* could endure. This government is believed to be strong because it is violent; but strength differs from violence as much as from weakness, and its astonishing manner of operation at the present time is perhaps enough proof that it cannot last very long. The French nation does not *want* this government, but *suffers* it, and remains submissive either because it cannot choke it off or because it fears something worse. The government rests on only two columns, neither of which possesses any reality; we may say that it rests entirely on two negations. We may also notice that the apologists of the Republic do not try to demonstrate its worthiness; they easily sense that this is the weak point in their armour. They say only, as boldly as they can, that its survival is a possibility, and passing lightly over this argument as over hot coals, they devote themselves solely to proving to the French that they will expose themselves to the greatest evils if they return to their old form of government. On this topic they are quite eloquent; they never stop talking about the dangers of revolution. If pressed, these people will admit to you that the Revolution that created the present government was a crime, provided that you grant them it is unnecessary to make a new one. They throw themselves on their knees

17. [Probably a reference to the Vendémiaire uprising (October 1795), which was in protest against the 'two-thirds' decree, whereby two-thirds of the members of the new assemblies of the Directory had to be chosen from among the members of the old Convention.]

before the French nation, they beg it to preserve the Republic. One senses in everything that they say about the stability of this government not reasoned conviction, but the dreams of desire.

Let us pass on to the great anathema that burdens the Republic.

V

The French Revolution Considered in Its Antireligious Character

Digression on Christianity

There is a satanic quality to the French Revolution that distinguishes it from everything we have ever seen or anything we are ever likely to see in the future. Recall the great assemblies, Robespierre's speech against the priesthood, the solemn apostasy of the clergy, the desecration of objects of worship, the installation of the goddess of reason, and that multitude of extraordinary actions by which the provinces sought to outdo Paris. All this goes beyond the ordinary circle of crime and seems to belong to another world.

Even now, when the Revolution has become less violent, and wanton excesses have disappeared, the principles remain. Have not the *legislators* (I use their term) passed the historically unique rule that the nation *will support no form of worship*?[1] Some of our contemporaries, it seems to

---

1. [A decree of 29 September 1795 on the exercise of worship.]

me, have at certain moments reached the point of hating the Divinity; but this frightful act of violence was not necessary to render the very greatest creative efforts useless. The mere omission (let alone contempt) of the great Being in any human endeavour brands it with an irrevocable anathema. Either every imaginable institution is founded on a religious concept or it is only a passing phenomenon. Institutions are strong and durable to the degree that they are, so to speak, *deified*. Not only is human reason, or what is ignorantly called *philosophy*, incapable of supplying these foundations, which with equal ignorance are called *superstitious*, but philosophy is, on the contrary, an essentially disruptive force.

In short, man cannot act the Creator without putting himself in harmony with Him. Mad as we are, if we want a mirror to reflect the image of the sun, would we turn it towards the earth?

These reflections are addressed to everyone, to the believer as well as to the sceptic; this is a fact that I advance and not a theory. Whether one laughs at religious ideas or venerates them does not matter; true or false, they nevertheless form the unique basis of all durable institutions.

Rousseau, perhaps the most self-deceived man who ever lived, nevertheless hit on this observation without wishing to draw the consequences from it.

'The Judaic Law,' he says, 'which is still in existence, and the Law of the child of Ishmael, which for ten centuries regulated the conduct of half the world, bear witness, even today, to the great men who gave them form. . . . Prideful philosophy or the blind spirit of party sees in them only lucky impostors.'[2] He had only to draw the logical conclusion from this, instead of talking to us of 'that great

2. *Contrat social*, Bk. II, ch. vii.

and powerful genius who watches over durable institutions',[3] as if this poetry explained anything.

When we reflect on the attested facts of all history, when we understand that in the chain of human institutions, from those that have marked the great turning points in history down to the smallest social organization, from empires down to brotherhoods, all have a divine foundation, and that human power, whenever it isolates itself, can only give its works a false and passing existence, what are we to think of the new French structure and the power that produced it? For myself, I will never believe in the fecundity of nothingness.

It would be curious to examine our European institutions one by one and to show how they are all *Christianized,* how religion mingles in everything, animates and sustains everything. Human passions may pollute and even pervert primitive creations, but if the principle is divine, this is enough to give them a prodigious permanence. The military orders are an example from among hundreds that might be cited.[4] Certainly it would imply no lack of respect for their members to affirm that the original religious objective may no longer be their primary concern. Nevertheless they continue to exist, and their longevity is a wonder. How many superficial wits laugh at this strange amalgam of monk and soldier? It would be better to go into ecstasies over the hidden force by which these orders have survived the centuries, overcoming formidable opponents and withstanding the most astounding assaults in history. Moreover, this force is the *name* on which these institutions are based, for nothing *is* only through *the one who is.* In the midst of

3. [Ibid.]
4. [The last of the great crusading orders, the Knights of Malta, was still in existence when Maistre wrote. It was suppressed in 1810.]

the general upheaval of which we are the witnesses, friends of order are especially disquieted by educational deficiencies. They are often heard to say that the Jesuits must be reestablished. Without disputing the merits of this order, one may say that this suggestion for their reestablishment indicates a lack of deep reflection. Do they mean that St. Ignatius is at hand ready to serve our purposes? If the order were destroyed, perhaps it could be reestablished by some lay brother with the same inspiration that created it originally, but all the sovereigns in the world would never succeed.[5]

5. [Maistre's original manuscript continued as follows: 'The more one examines things closely, the more one will be convinced that the social edifice rests entirely on the cross and that what still saves us from a general upheaval is that the various governments in this part of the world, perhaps by instinct and habit rather than by conviction or wisdom, continue to maintain the religious establishment. In France, the culpable foolishness of the government having favoured the spread of impiety or indifference become too generalized, we see the consequences.

'Whenever education ceases to be religious, there is no longer national education. You will still make mathematicians, physicists, etc., but it is a question of making men. Moreover, a proper system of education to create real public spirit will be religious or it will not accomplish anything.

'Religion surrounds us on all sides; everything speaks its language to us. Its characters are imprinted on our flags, our coinage, our medals of honour, our ornaments, our buildings, and all our monuments. It animates, vivifies, perpetuates, and infuses our legislation. It sanctions our customs; it presides over our treaties. It has formed the great European family. Its gentle laws calmed our ferocity and helped unite our divergent spirits. From St. Petersburg to Madrid, people made contracts in the name of the very holy and indivisible trinity. It was the great family title and the proof of a common kinship. The hideous hand of revolutionary genius came to efface this sacred formula, and it has destroyed . . .']

This is a divine law as certain and as palpable as the laws of motion. Every time a man puts himself, according to his abilities, in harmony with the Creator and produces any institution whatsoever in the name of the Divinity, then no matter what his individual weaknesses, ignorance, poverty, obscurity of birth, in short, his absolute lack of ordinary human resources, he participates in some manner in the power whose instrument he has made himself. He produces works whose strength and permanence astonish reason.

I ask every attentive reader of good will to look around him, for he will find these great truths demonstrated in even the smallest examples. One need not go back to the *son of Ishmael*, to Lycurgus, to Numa, or to Moses, whose laws were entirely religious; a popular festival, a rustic dance, will suffice for the observant. We still see in some Protestant countries certain gatherings, certain popular occasions that no longer have any apparent reason but that come down from Catholic usages which have been completely forgotten. Holidays of this kind have nothing moral, nothing respectable in themselves; it makes no difference, for they derive, however remotely, from religious ideas, and this is enough to perpetuate them. Three centuries have not been able to erase their memory.

But you, masters of the earth—princes, kings, emperors, powerful majesties, invincible conquerors—simply try to make the people go on such-and-such a day each year to a given place to dance. I ask little of you, but I dare give you a solemn challenge to succeed, whereas the humblest missionary will succeed and be obeyed two thousand years after his death. Every year the people gather around some rustic temple in the name of St. John, St. Martin, St. Benedict, etc.; they come, animated by a feverish and yet innocent eagerness; religion sanctifies their joy and the joy embellishes religion; they forget their troubles; on leaving they think of the pleasure that they will have on the same day the following year, and the date is set in their minds.[6]

Beside this picture, put that of the masters of France, who have been invested with every power by an unprecedented revolution and who are unable to organize a simple holiday. They pour out money, they call all the arts to their assistance, and the citizens remain at home, taking notice of the call only to laugh at the organizers. Listen to this description of impotence. Listen to the memorable words of one of these *deputies of the people* speaking at a session of the Convention in January 1796:[7] 'What then! Men foreign to our ways, our usages, have been able to establish ridiculous feasts for unknown events, to honour men whose very existence is problematic. What! They have been able to secure the employment of immense funds for the dull daily repetition of insignificant and often absurd ceremonies. And the men who have overthrown the Bastille and the throne, the men who have defeated Europe, will not succeed in preserving by national holidays the memory of the great events that immortalize our revolution.'

Delirium! The depths of human weakness! Legislators, meditate on this great admission that teaches you what you are and what you can do. Now what more do you need to judge the French system? If its nullity is not clear, nothing is certain in this world.

I am so convinced of the truths I defend that when I consider the general weakening of moral principles, the

6. 'Let them limit those public displays provided for the entertainment of the populace to singing and instrumental recitals . . . and thus let them render that delight consonant with the honour of the gods.' Cicero, *De Legibus*, II, 9.

7. [Maistre gives the wrong date; the discussion in question took place in 1795.]

divergence of opinions, the shaking of spineless monarchies, the immensity of our needs, and the poverty of our means, it seems to me that all true philosophy must opt between these two hypotheses: either a new religion is going to come into existence or Christianity will be rejuvenated in some extraordinary way. You must choose between these two suppositions according to the position you have taken on the truth of Christianity.

This conjecture will be scornfully rejected only by those shortsighted men who believe only what they can see. Who in antiquity could have foreseen Christianity? And in its beginnings, what man unfamiliar with this religion could have foreseen its success? How do we know that a great moral revolution has not already begun? Pliny, as his famous letter proves, had not the slightest appreciation of the giant whose infancy he witnessed.[8]

But a crowd of ideas overwhelms me at this point and pushes me to the very broadest considerations.

The present generation is witnessing one of the greatest spectacles ever beheld by human eyes; it is the fight to the death between Christianity and philosophism.[9] The lists are open, the two enemies have come to grips, and the world looks on. As in Homer, *the father of gods and men* is holding the balance in which these two great causes are being weighed; one of the scales will soon descend.

To the prejudiced man, and especially to the one whose heart has convinced his head, events prove nothing; he having taken one side or the other irrevocably, observation and reasoning are equally useless. But all you men of good

8. [Pliny the Younger (62–120), named governor of Bithynia, wrote to the Emperor Trajan to ask him what attitude to take towards the Christians.]

9. [Maistre used the word *philosophisme* to refer to the philosophy of the philosophes.]

faith who may deny or doubt what I say, perhaps the great example of Christianity will settle your uncertainty. For eighteen centuries it has ruled a great part of the world, particularly the most enlightened portion of the globe. This religion even predates antiquity, for it is linked through its founder to another order of things, to an archetypal religion, that preceded it. The one cannot be true without the other being so; the one boasts of promising what the other boasts of having, so that this religion, by a chain that is a visible fact, goes back to the beginning of the world: *It was born the day the days were born.*[10]

Such duration is without example, and even taking Christianity by itself, no institution in the world can match it. To compare it to other religions is mere wrangling; several striking characteristics exclude all comparison. This is not the place to list them; just a word will be enough. Who can show us one other religion founded on miracles and revealing incomprehensible dogmas, yet believed for eighteen centuries by the greater part of mankind and defended down through the ages by the greatest men of each era from Origen[11] to Pascal, despite the utmost efforts of an enemy sect that, from Celsus[12] to Condorcet, has never ceased its bellowing?

How remarkable that when we reflect on this institution, the most natural hypothesis, the one suggested by every

10. [Maistre used the same line, *Elle naquit le jour où naquirent les jours*, in a memoir on Freemasonry which he wrote in 1782. See *La Franc-Maçonnerie: Mémoire inédit au duc de Brunswick*, ed. E. Dermenghem (Paris: Rieder, 1925). I have been unable to find its source.]

11. [Origen (185–254) was an early Father of the Church whose brilliant, but occasionally heterodox, writings Maistre greatly admired.]

12. [Celsus was a second-century Platonist celebrated for his attacks on Christianity.]

probability, is that of divine origin! If this is a human creation there is no longer any way to explain its success; by excluding the miracle you require more miracles.

They say that the nations have mistaken copper for gold. Very well, but has this copper been thrown into the European crucible and been subject to chemical observation for eighteen centuries? And is the result of this test in its favour? Newton believed in the Incarnation, but Plato, I think, put little stock in the miraculous birth of Bacchus. Christianity has been preached by the ignorant and believed by the scholars, and in this respect it is absolutely unique.

Moreover, it has survived every test. They say that persecution is a wind that nourishes and spreads the flame of fanaticism. Very well, Diocletian favoured Christianity; but by this supposition Constantine should have stifled it, but this is not what happened. It has withstood everything— peace, war, scaffolds, triumphs, daggers, temptations, pride, humiliation, affluence, the night of the Middle Ages, and the bright daylight of the centuries of Leo X and Louis XIV. An all-powerful emperor, master of the greatest part of the known world, once used all the resources of his genius against it.[13] He omitted nothing in his attempt to revive the ancient beliefs, cleverly associating them with the Platonic ideas then in fashion. Hiding the rage that animated him under a mask of purely external tolerance, he used against the rival cult arms that no human creation had ever resisted: he exposed it to ridicule, impoverished its priesthood to bring it into contempt, and deprived it of every assistance that man is able to give his works; defamation, intrigues, injustice, oppression, ridicule, force, and

13. [This is a reference to Julian the Apostate, who though raised a Christian, tried to reestablish paganism when he became emperor.]

cunning were all useless. The *Galilean* triumphed over Julian, *the philosophe.*

And finally, in our own time, the experiment is being repeated in still more favourable circumstances, and nothing is lacking to make it decisive. So pay close attention, all you for whom history has not been instruction enough. You say that the sceptre supported the tiara. Very well! The sceptre no longer counts on the world's stage; it has been broken and the pieces thrown in the mud. You wondered to what extent a rich and powerful priesthood could influence acceptance of the dogmas that it preached. I do not believe that it really had the power to make people believe, but let that pass. There are no longer any priests; they have been exiled, slaughtered, and debased; they have been despoiled, and those who have escaped the guillotine, the stake, daggers, fusillades, drownings, and deportation today receive the alms that formerly they themselves gave. You feared the force of custom, the ascendancy of authority, the illusions of the imagination. None of these things are left; there are no more customs, there are no more masters, each man's mind is his own. Philosophy having corroded the cement that united men, there are no longer any moral bonds. The civil authority, favouring with all its strength the overthrow of the old system, gives to the enemies of Christianity all the support that it once gave to Christianity itself. Every means imaginable to the human mind is used to combat the old national religion. These efforts are applauded and rewarded, and contrary efforts are regarded as crimes. There is no longer any reason to fear visual delights, always the first to deceive; displays of pomp and vain ceremonies no longer impress men before whom everything has been mocked for seven years. The churches are closed, or open only for the feverish discussions and drunken revels of an unbridled populace. The altars are overthrown, filthy animals have been paraded through the streets in bishop's vestments, chalices have been used in abominable orgies, and on the altars that the old faith surrounded with dazzling cherubim they have placed nude prostitutes. Philosophism no longer has any complaints to make; all the human chances are in its favour; everything has been done for it and against its rival. If it wins, it will not say like Caesar, *I came, I saw, I conquered*, but in the end it will have conquered; it can applaud and sit proudly on an overturned cross. But if Christianity emerges from this terrible ordeal purer and more vigorous, if the Christian Hercules, strong in his own strength, lifts up the son of the earth and crushes him in his arms, *patuit Deus*.[14] Frenchmen, make way for the very Christian king, carry him yourselves to his ancient throne, raise again his oriflamme, and let his coinage, ranging again from one pole to the other, carry everywhere the triumphant device

CHRIST COMMANDS, HE REIGNS,

HE IS THE VICTOR!

14. [God is open.]

VI

On Divine Influence in Political Constitutions

Man can modify everything within the sphere of his activity, but he creates nothing: such is his law, in the physical world as in the moral world.

Undoubtedly a man may plant a seed, raise the tree, perfect it by grafting, and trim it a hundred different ways, but he would never imagine that he had the power to make a tree. How can he have imagined that he had the power to make a constitution? Would it be from experience? Let us see what experience teaches us.

All free constitutions known to men have been formed in one of two ways. Sometimes they have *germinated*, as it were, in an unconscious manner through the conjunction of a multitude of so-called fortuitous circumstances, and sometimes they have a single author, who appears like a sport of nature and enforces obedience. In either case, here are the signs by which God warns us of our weakness and of the rights that He has reserved to Himself in the formation of governments:

1. No constitution is the result of deliberation. The rights of the people are never written, or at any rate, constitutive acts or fundamental written laws are never more than declaratory statements of anterior rights about which nothing can be said except that they exist because they exist.[1]

2. God, not having judged it appropriate to use supernatural means in this area, has at least so far circumscribed human action that in the formation of constitutions circumstances do everything and men are only part of the circumstances. Commonly enough, even in pursuing one goal they attain another, as we have seen in the English constitution.

3. The rights of the *people*, properly so called, often enough proceed from the concessions of sovereigns and in this case can be verified historically; but the rights of the monarch and the aristocracy, at least their essential rights, those which we may call constitutive and *basic*, have neither date nor author.

4. Even these concessions of the sovereign have always been preceded by a state of affairs that made them necessary and that did not depend on him.

5. Although written laws are merely declarations of anterior rights, it is far from true that everything can be written down; in fact there are always some things in every constitution that cannot be written and that must be allowed to remain in dark and reverent obscurity on pain of upsetting the state.[2]

---

1. 'It would take a fool to ask who gave liberty to the cities of Sparta, Rome, etc. These republics did not receive their charters from men. God and nature gave them to them.' Sidney, *Disc. sur le gouv.*, I, 2. The author is not suspect. [Algernon Sidney, *Discourses concerning Government* (London: 1698).]

2. The wise Hume often noticed this. I will cite only the following passage: 'This [Parliament's right to remonstrate against the

6. The more that is written, the weaker the institution becomes, and the reason for this is clear. Laws are only declarations of rights, and rights are declared only when they are attacked, so that a multiplicity of written constitutional laws proves only a multiplicity of conflicts and the danger of destruction.

This is why the most vigorous political system of secular antiquity was that of Sparta, in which nothing was written.

7. No nation can give itself liberty if it is not already free.[3] When a nation begins to reflect on its existence, its laws are already made. Human influence does not extend beyond the development of rights already existing but disregarded or disputed. If imprudent men overstep these limits with reckless reforms, the nation will lose what rights it had without attaining those it hopes for. From this follows the necessity of innovating only rarely and always with moderation and trepidation.

8. When Providence decrees the more rapid formation of a political constitution, there appears a man invested with an indefinable power: he speaks and makes himself obeyed. But these marvellous men belong perhaps only to the world of antiquity and to the youth of nations. Whatever the case, the distinctive characteristic of these legislators par excel-

---

king] touched upon that circumstance in the English constitution which is most difficult, or rather altogether impossible, to regulate by laws, and which must be governed by certain delicate ideas of propriety and decency, rather than to any exact rule or prescription.' Hume, *History of England*, *Charles I*, ch. lvi, note B. Thomas Payne [*sic*], as we know, is of another opinion. He claims that a constitution does not exist unless he can put it in his pocket.

3. 'A people that has been accustomed to live under a prince preserves its liberties with difficulty, if by accident it has become free.' Machiavelli, *Discources on Titus Livy*, Bk. I, ch. xvi.

lence is that they are kings or high nobles; there never has been nor can there ever be any exception to this.

This is why Solon's constitution was the most fragile of antiquity.[4] Athens' days of glory, which were so ephemeral,[5] were soon ended by conquest and tyranny, and Solon himself lived to see the Pisistratids.[6]

9. Even these legislators, notwithstanding their extraordinary power, only combine preexisting elements in the customs and character of a people; and this gathering together, this rapid formation that resembles creation, is accomplished only in the name of the Divinity. The polity and the religion are founded together; the legislator is scarcely distinguishable from the priest, and his public institutions consist principally in *ceremonies and religious holidays*.[7]

10. In one sense, liberty has always been the gift of kings,[8] for all free nations were established by kings. This is

4. Plutarch clearly recognized this truth. 'Solon', he said, 'could not maintain a city in union and concord for long . . . because he had been born of ordinary stock, and not of the city's wealthiest, so of middle class only.' *Life of Solon*, Amyot's translation.

5. 'The era of Athenian generals came to an end with Iphicrates, Chabrias, and Timotheus, and after the death of those eminent men no general in that city was worthy of notice.' Cornelius Nepos, *Life of Timotheus*, ch. iv. From the battle of Marathon to that of Leucade won by Timothy was only 114 years. That was the compass of the glory of Athens.

6. [Pisistratus and then his sons succeeded Solon as tyrants of Athens.]

7. Plutarch, *Life of Numa*.

8. 'Nor is there any doubt that the same Brutus who earned such honour by expelling the haughty Tarquinius would have acted in an evil hour for the commonwealth had a premature eagerness for liberty led him to wrest power from any of the earlier kings.' Titus Livy, II, 1. The entire passage is well worth meditation.

the general rule, and the exceptions that may be mentioned would also fall under the rule if they were examined closely.

11. There has never been a free nation that did not have in its natural constitution seeds of liberty as old as itself, nor has any nation, by writing constitutional laws, ever succeeded in developing rights other than those in its natural constitution.

12. No mere assembly of men can form a nation, and the very attempt exceeds in folly the most absurd and extravagant things that all the Bedlams of the world might put forth.[9]

To prove this proposition in detail, after what I said, would, it seems to me, be lacking in respect to the knowledgeable and paying too much honour to the ignorant.

13. I have spoken of one basic characteristic of true legislators. Another very remarkable feature, on which it would be easy to write a book, is that they are never what are called scholars: they do not write, they act on instinct and impulse more than on reasoning, and they have no other means of acting than a certain moral force that bends men's wills like grain before the wind.

I could say some interesting things in showing that this observation is only the corollary of a general truth of the highest importance, but I am afraid I digress. I would rather omit the intermediary arguments and pass on to the conclusions.

There is the same difference between political theory and constitutional laws as there is between poetics and poetry. The illustrious Montesquieu is to Lycurgus, in the intel-

---

9. 'It is even necessary that he whose mind has conceived a constitution should be alone in carrying it into effect.' Machiavelli, *Discourses on Titus Livy*, Bk. I, ch. ix.

lectual hierarchy, what Batteux[10] is to Homer or Racine. Moreover, these two talents positively exclude each other, as can be seen by the example of Locke, who fumbled badly when he presumed to give laws to the Americans.[11]

I have heard a great supporter of the Republic seriously lamenting that the French had not found in Hume's works a piece entitled *Plan for a Perfect Republic. O coecas hominum mentes.*[12] If you see an ordinary man of good sense who has never shown in any way any external sign of superiority, you cannot be sure that he would not be a good legislator. There is no reason to say yes or no. But if it is a question of Bacon, Locke, or Montesquieu, etc., you can say no without hesitation, for the one talent they do possess proves that they do not have the other.[13]

The application to the French constitution of the principles that I have just stated follows naturally; but it is well to look at the matter from a particular viewpoint.

The greatest enemies of the French Revolution must frankly admit that the commission of eleven that produced the last constitution would appear to have had more sense than its work, and it perhaps did everything that could have been done. Working with recalcitrant materials, it was not able to follow principles, but the division of powers alone, even though the division is only that of a wall,[14] is

10. [Charles Batteux (1713–80) was a grammarian and translator who published an edition of Aristotle's *Poetics*.]

11. [As secretary to the earl of Shaftesbury, one of the proprietors of Carolina, Locke helped his patron draw up the Fundamental Constitutions of the colony in 1669. This constitution was rejected by the colonists in 1693.]

12. [Oh how blind are the minds of men.]

13. Plato, Zeno, and Chrysippus made books, but Lycurgus acted (Plutarch, *Life of Lycurgus*). There is not a single sane idea in morals or politics that escaped Plutarch's good sense.

14. 'Under no circumstances may the two Councils meet in one and the same hall.' *Constitution de 1795*, Title V, article 60.

nevertheless a fine victory over the prejudices of the moment.

But it is not only a question of the intrinsic merits of the constitution. My intention does not include investigating the particular faults that assure us that it cannot last; besides, everything has been said on this point. I will only indicate the theoretical error that has served as the basis for this constitution and that has misled the French from the very beginning of their revolution.

The Constitution of 1795, like its predecessors, was made for *man*. But there is no such thing as *man* in the world. In my lifetime I have seen Frenchmen, Italians, Russians, etc.; thanks to Montesquieu, I even know that *one can be Persian*. But as for *man*, I declare that I have never in my life met him; if he exists, he is unknown to me.

Is there a single country in the world where you can find a Council of Five Hundred, a Council of Elders, and five Directors? This constitution might be offered to any human association from China to Geneva. But a constitution that is made for all nations is made for none; it is a pure abstraction, an academic exercise made according to some hypothetical ideal, which should be addressed to *man* in his imaginary dwelling place.

What is a constitution? Is it not merely the solution of the following problem? *Given the population, the mores, the religion, the geographic situation, the political circumstances, the wealth, the good and the bad qualities of a particular nation, to find the laws that suit it.*

Now the Constitution of 1795, which treats only of man, does not grapple with this problem at all.

Thus every imaginable reason combines to prove that this work does not possess the divine seal. It is only a *school composition.*

Consequently, already at this moment, how many signs of decay!

VII

Evidence of the Incapacity of the Present French Government

A legislator resembles the Creator by not working all the time; he creates and then he rests. All true legislative action has its *Sabbath*, and intermittence is its distinctive characteristic. Ovid thus announced a truth of the first order when he said *Quod caret alterna requie durabile non est*.[1]

If perfection were an attribute of human nature, each legislator would speak only once; but since all our works are imperfect, in the measure that political institutions deteriorate, the sovereign is obliged to support them with new laws. Nevertheless, human legislation should resemble its model by this intermittence of which I have just spoken. As honoured by its repose as by its original action, the more it acts, the more human and the more fragile its work.

Look at the labours of the three French national assemblies. What a prodigious number of laws!

1. Ovid, *Heroides*, IV, 89. [That which lacks its alternations of repose will not endure.]

From 1 July 1789 to October 1791, the
National Assembly passed   2,557

The Legislative Assembly, in 11½
months, passed   1,712

The National Convention, from the first
day of the Republic to 4 Brumaire
of the Year IV (26 October 1795),
passed in 57 months   11,210

     $\overline{}$

     15,479[2]

I doubt that the three French royal houses ever produced such a collection. When one reflects on this infinite number of laws, one experiences in turn two very different sentiments. The first is that of admiration or at least astonishment. With Mr. Burke, one is surprised that this nation, whose levity is proverbial, has produced such obstinate workers.[3] Such a structure of laws is a stupefying monument of Atlantean proportions. But astonishment immediately becomes pity when one thinks of the nullity of these laws, and one sees mere children killing each other to build a house of cards.

Why so many laws? Because there is no legislator. What have these so-called legislators done in six years? Nothing, for *to destroy* is not *to make*.

2. This calculation, which was made in France, is reported in a foreign gazette for February 1796. This number of 15,479 in less than six years appeared to me to be honest enough, when I found in my notes the assertion from one of those scintillating sheets (*Quotidienne*, 30 November 1796, no. 218) by a very pleasant journalist who was absolutely sure that the French republic possessed two million and some hundreds of thousands of printed laws and eighteen hundred thousand that are not printed. I will not argue the point.

3. [Probably a reference to Edmund Burke's *Reflections on the Revolution in France*, a work that Maistre read and admired.]

It is hard to imagine the unbelievable spectacle of a nation giving itself three constitutions in five years. A real legislator does not fumble around; he says *fiat* and the machine goes. Despite the various efforts the three assemblies have made in this matter, everything has gone from bad to worse since the assent of the nation to the work of the legislators has been steadily decreasing.

Certainly the Constitution of 1791 was a vain monument to folly; nevertheless, it must be admitted that it enthralled the French and that the majority of the nation wholeheartedly, if foolishly, swore an oath to *the nation, the law, and the king*. The French were so taken with this constitution that even after it was no longer a practical question, it was common enough to hear them argue *that in order to return to the real monarchy it would be necessary to go back to the Constitution of 1791*. Which is really equivalent to saying that to return to Europe from Asia it is necessary to go by way of the moon; but I am merely setting out the facts.[4]

Condorcet's constitution was never tested and was never worth trying;[5] the one that was preferred, the work of a

---

4. An intelligent man who had his reasons for praising that constitution and who was very sure that it was a *monument of written reason* nevertheless agreed that, without mentioning the horror of two chambers and the restriction of the *veto*, it contained *several other anarchical principles* (20 or 30 for example). See *Coup d'oeil sur la Revolution française, par un ami de l'ordre et des lois*, by M. M. [General Montesquiou], Hamburg, 1794, pages 28 and 77.

But what follows is even more curious. *This constitution*, the author says, *sins not by what it includes but by what it lacks.* Ibid., p. 27. Which is to say that the Constitution of 1791 would have been perfect if it had been made; this is the Apollo of the Belvedere, less the statue and the pedestal.

5. [Condorcet was the reporter for a constitutional committee named by the Convention in October 1792.]

few cutthroats,[6] still pleases similar men, and this phalanx, thanks to the Revolution, is numerous enough in France. So all things considered, of the three, the present constitution has the fewest supporters. In the primary assemblies that accepted it (according to the government) many members naively wrote, *accepted for want of something better*. This in effect is the general disposition of the nation: people submit through lassitude, through despair of finding anything better. Overwhelmed by an excess of misfortunes, they thought they could gain a breathing spell under this frail tree; they preferred a bad port to an angry sea. But nowhere does one sense conviction or sincere consent. If this constitution really suited the French, the invisible efficacy of experience would be winning new supporters every day; but what is happening is precisely the opposite. Democracy loses a new deserter every minute. Fear and apathy are all that guard the Pentarchy's throne,[7] and the most clairvoyant and disinterested travellers who have been to France all agree that *it is a republic without republicans*.

But if, as has been so often preached to kings, the strength of a government resides entirely in the love of its subjects, if fear alone is an insufficient means of main-

6. [After the expulsion of the Girondins by the radical Jacobins in early June 1793, five Jacobins were added to the constitutional committee. The result of the committee's labours was the Constitution of the Year II, which was adopted by the Convention on 24 June 1793. However, the implementation of this constitution, which was the most democratic of the Revolution, was postponed because of the emergency situation, and finally forgotten. The Constitution of 1795, a much more conservative document, was drawn up in the closing months of the Convention.]

7. [Maistre's reference is to the five Directors who formed the executive of the government.]

taining sovereignty, what must we think of the French Republic?

Open your eyes and you will see that it does not *live*. What an enormous machine! What a multiplicity of springs and clockwork! What a fracas of pieces clanging away! What an immense number of men employed to repair the damage! Everything tells us there is nothing natural in these movements, for the primary characteristic of the creations of nature is power accompanied by an economy of means. Everything being in its place, there are no jerks or bumps, friction is low, and there is no noise, only majestic silence. So it is that in the mechanism of nature, perfect balance, equilibrium, and exact symmetry of parts give even rapid movement the satisfying appearance of repose.

Therefore sovereignty does not exist in France. Everything is artificial and violent, and it all announces that such an order of things cannot last.

Modern philosophy is at the same time too materialistic and too presumptuous to perceive the real mainsprings of the political world. One of its follies is to believe that an assembly can constitute a nation, that a *constitution*, that is to say, the totality of fundamental laws that are proper to a nation and that give it such-and-such a form of government, is an artifact like any other, requiring only intelligence, knowledge, and practice, that one can learn the *trade of constitution-making*, and that any day they think about it, men may say to other men, *make us a government*, as they say to a workman, *make us a steam pump or a stocking frame*.

Nevertheless, it is a truth as certain in its way as a mathematical proposition that no great institution results from deliberation and that human works are fragile in proportion to the number of men involved in their construction and to the degree to which science and reasoning have been employed a priori.

A written constitution, such as that which rules the French today, is only an automaton possessing merely the exterior appearance of life. Man, by his own powers, is at most a Vaucanson; to be a Prometheus, he must climb to heaven, for *the legislator cannot gain obedience either by force or by reasoning.*[8]

At the moment, the experiment may be said to be over, for to say that the constitution is working would be inattentively to mistake the constitution for the government. The latter, which is a highly advanced despotism, works only too well, but the constitution exists only on paper. It is observed or violated according to the interests of the rulers; the people count for nothing, and the insults that their masters address to them under the forms of respect are well suited to cure them of their errors.

The life of a government is something as real as the life of a man; one senses it, or better, one sees it, and no one is deceived on this point. I beseech every Frenchman who has a conscience to ask himself if it does not take some effort to give his representatives the title of *legislators*, if this title of etiquette and *courtesy* does not cost him the kind of effort he experienced when, under the old regime, he was pleased to call the son of a royal secretary *count* or *marquis?*[9]

All honour comes from God, said Homer of old;[10] he spoke exactly like St. Paul, without having plagiarized him.

8. Rousseau, *Contrat social*, Bk. II, ch. vii.
9. [Anyone with enough money could purchase the office of royal secretary (*Secrétaire du Roi*), which carried with it hereditary nobility. The office was despised by the older nobility because it demeaned their own status.]
10. *Iliad*, I, 178.

One thing certain is that man cannot impart that indefinable characteristic that is called *dignity*. *Honour* belongs preeminently to the sovereign alone; from him, as from an immense reservoir, it is bestowed in proper number, weight, and measure on various classes and individuals.

I notice that when a member of the legislature spoke of his RANK in a pamphlet, the newspapers mocked him, because in effect there is no *rank* in France, but only *power*, which merely depends on force. The people see a deputy as only the seven-hundred-and-fiftieth part of a power capable of doing a great deal of harm. A deputy is respected not because he is a *deputy* but because he is respectable. Everyone would undoubtedly like to have given M. Siméon's speech on divorce, but everyone wishes that he had given it before a legitimate assembly.[11]

Perhaps it is an illusion on my part, but this *wage* that a vainglorious neologism calls an indemnity seems to me to prejudice the French system of representation. The Englishman, free by law and independent by fortune, who comes to London to represent the nation at his own expense, has something imposing about him. But these French *legislators* who charge the nation five or six million livres to make laws for it, these *decree-sellers* who exercise the national sovereignty for eight myriagrammes of grain per day and who live off their legislative power—such men are not, in truth, very impressive, and when one comes to ask

11. [Joseph-Jérôme Siméon (1749–1842), a former law professor who had lost his post during the Revolution for his opposition to the Civil Constitution of the Clergy, was elected to the Council of Five Hundred during the Directory. His speech to the Council of Elders, 24 January 1797, argued that divorce introduced a kind of prostitution. Arrested in the coup d'état of Fructidor, Siméon survived to fill important positions under subsequent regimes.]

what they are worth, the imagination cannot help evaluating them in wheat.

In England, these two magic letters, M.P., added to a little-known name suddenly exalt it and give it the right to a distinguished marriage. In France, a man who would intrigue for a deputy's place in order to gain an otherwise unlikely marriage would most probably be reckoning poorly. This is because any representative, any instrument whatever, of a false sovereignty can excite only curiosity or terror.

Such is the incredible weakness of isolated human power that it is not even capable of establishing a style of dress. How many reports were made to the Legislative Assembly on the costumes of its members? Three or four at least, but it was always in vain. Pictures of these beautiful costumes are sold in foreign countries, while in Paris public opinion ridicules them.

An ordinary costume, contemporaneous with a great event, can be consecrated by that event; it will then have a mark of distinction that will sustain it in the world of fashion. While other styles change, it will remain the same, always respected. This is more or less the way that costumes of great dignity originate.

For those who notice all sorts of things, it may be interesting to observe that of all the revolutionary finery, the only items that have had a consistent popularity are the sash and plume, and these come from chivalry. These survive, although blighted like trees from which the nourishing sap has been cut off but which have not yet lost their beauty. The *public official* laden with these dishonoured symbols is something like a robber conspicuous in the clothes of the man he has just stripped.

I am not sure how well I read, but I read the nullity of this government everywhere. Conquests by the French have drawn a great deal of attention and created illusions about the prospects of their government; even the best minds are dazzled by the glamour of these military successes, and so they do not at first perceive to what degree these successes have nothing to do with the stability of the Republic.

Nations have conquered under all possible forms of government, and even revolutions, by exalting morale, may lead to victories. The French will always succeed in war when under a firm government that has the wit to praise them while despising them and that throws them at the enemy like bullets while promising them epitaphs in the newspapers.

Even now it is still Robespierre who is winning the battles; it is his iron despotism that leads the French to butchery and victory. It is by squandering gold and blood, it is by straining every resource that the masters of France have obtained the successes we witness. A superlatively brave nation exalted by any kind of fanaticism, and led by able generals, will always conquer, but it will pay dearly for its conquests. Did the Constitution of 1793 receive the seal of longevity from its three years of victory? Why should it be otherwise for that of 1795, and why should victory give this one a character that it was unable to give the other?

Moreover, a nation's character always remains the same. Barclay, in the sixteenth century, succinctly described the military character of France. 'It is a nation', he said, 'supremely brave and invincible on its own soil; but when it expands beyond its borders it is quite another thing. This is why it has never been able to retain dominion over foreign peoples and why its strength is its own misfortune.'[12]

No one feels more strongly than I that the present

12. J. Barclaius, *Icon Animorum*, cap. III. [John Barclay (1582–1621) was an English writer best known for his controversy with Bellarmine over the power of the pope.]

circumstances are extraordinary and that it is very possible that what has always happened before will not happen this time; but this question is irrelevant to the purpose of this work. It suffices for me to indicate the falsity of the argument that *the republic is victorious, therefore it will last.* If it were absolutely necessary to prophesy, I would rather say that *war keeps it alive, therefore peace will kill it.*

The inventor of a system of physics would undoubtedly congratulate himself if he had all the facts of nature in his favour; I can cite in support of my reflections all the facts of history. Examining in good faith all the examples history furnishes us, I see nothing favouring this chimerical system of deliberation and political construction by abstract reasoning. At the most one could mention America, but I have replied in advance to this by saying that the time has not yet come to cite it. I will, however, add a few comments.

1. British America had a king but never saw him; the splendour of monarchy was foreign to it, and its sovereign was a kind of supernatural power that was never really felt.

2. It possessed the democratic element that existed in the constitution of the mother country.

3. It possessed, besides, those democratic elements that were carried hither by a multitude of its early colonists, who were born amid political and religious troubles and were almost all republican-minded.

4. The Americans built with these elements and on the plan of three powers that they received from their ancestors, and not at all *tabula rasa,* as the French did.

But all those things that are really new in their government, all those things that are the result of popular deliberation, are the most fragile parts of the system; one could scarcely combine more symptoms of weakness and decay.

Not only do I doubt the stability of the American government, but the particular establishments of English America inspire no confidence in me. The cities, for example, animated by a hardly respectable jealousy, have not been able to agree as to where the Congress should meet; none of them wanted to concede the honour to another. In consequence, they have decided to build a new city to be the capital. They have chosen a very favourable location on the banks of a great river and decreed that the city should be called *Washington*. The sites of all the public buildings have been marked out, the work has begun, and the plan of this queen city has already made the rounds in Europe. Essentially there is nothing in all this that surpasses human power; a city may easily be built. Nevertheless, there is too much deliberation, too much *humanity* in this business, and one could bet a thousand to one that the city will not be built, that it will not be called *Washington*, and that the Congress will not meet there.

VIII

Of the Old
French Constitution

Digression on the king and on his
declaration to the French of July 1795[1]

People have held different theories about the old French constitution: some have claimed that the nation had no constitution; others have claimed the contrary; and finally,

1. [Louis XVIII's Declaration of Verona, issued in July 1795, after the prison death of Louis XVI's son, appeared hopelessly reactionary to contemporary French republicans and most moderate royalists. He called for punishment for the regicides responsible for Louis XVI's death (about half of the members of the Convention), return to the old constitution of an hereditary monarchy (but with a reform of abuses), reestablishment of Catholicism as the religion of state (though with toleration for other religions), restoration of the parlements as guardians of the law, reconstitution of the three Estates, and convocation of an Estates-General that might vote new taxes and present its petitions to the king (but the king would retain the right to dismiss it). The declaration did not mention the confiscated property of the Church and the émigré nobles, but most people assumed that Louis' intentions were to restore this property to its former owners.]

others, taking a middle position, as usually happens on important questions, have claimed that the French really had a constitution, but that it was not observed.

The error of those who claim that France had no constitution stems from that great mistake about human power, prior deliberation and written laws.

If a man of good faith, given only good sense and probity, were to ask what the old French constitution was, he could be answered boldly: 'It is what you sensed when you were in France; it is that mixture of liberty and authority, law and opinion that would lead the foreign traveller in France, even though he was subject to a monarchy in his own country, to believe that he was now living under another government than his own.'

But if one wants to study the question more deeply, the characteristics and laws which ranked France above all known monarchies may be found in the corpus of French public law.

This monarchy possesses a certain theocratic element that is peculiarly its own and that has given it a lifespan of fourteen hundred years. There is nothing so national as this element. The bishops, successors to the Druids in this respect, only perfected it.

I do not believe that any other European monarchy has employed, for the good of the state, a greater number of priests in its civil government. I think back to the pacific Fleury, to the Saint-Ouens, to the Saint-Legers,[2] and many others so distinguished for their political sense in the troubles of their times, veritable Orpheuses of France who

2. [Cardinal Fleury was first minister in the early years (1726–43) of Louis XV's reign; Saint-Leger (616–78), bishop of Autun, was a councillor during the minority of Clotaire III; and Saint-Ouen (605–83), a bishop of Rouen, was chancellor under Dagobert I.]

tamed the tigers and made them follow in chains. I doubt whether one could find a parallel series anywhere.

But while the priesthood in France was one of the three pillars supporting the throne and played such an important role in the nation's councils, tribunals, ministries, and consulates, it had no influence, or very little influence, in civil administration, and even when a priest was first minister, France never had a 'government of priests'.

Every influence was well balanced and everyone had his place. From this point of view it is England that most resembles France. If England ever banished the words *Church and State* from its political vocabulary, its government would perish just like that of its rival.

It was the fashion in France (for everything is a matter of fashion in that country) to say that Frenchmen were slaves; but why then was the word *citoyen*, a word that cannot be translated into other European languages, found in the French language even before the Revolution took it up in order to dishonour it? The younger Racine addressed this beautiful verse to the king of France in the name of his city of Paris: *Under a citizen king, every citizen is king.*

To praise a Frenchman's patriotism, one said *C'est un grand citoyen.* It is hopeless to try to use this expression in our other languages. *Gross bürger* in German,[3] *gran cittadino* in Italian, etc., are simply not tolerable.[4] But we must go beyond generalities.

3. *Bürger: verbum humile apud nos et ignobile.* J. A. Ernesti, in *Dedicat, Opp. Ciceronii,* p. 79. [Bürger: a word which appears base and undistinguished.]

4. Rousseau has an absurd note on this word *citoyen* in his *Contrat social,* Bk. I, ch. vi. He thoughtlessly accuses a very knowledgeable man (Bodin) of having made a clumsy blunder on this point, and Jean-Jacques makes clumsy blunders in every

Several members of the old magistracy have collected and developed the principles of the French monarchy in an interesting book that would appear to merit the confidence of the French.[5]

These magistrates begin, as is proper, with the royal prerogative, and certainly there is nothing finer. 'The constitution attributes the legislative power to the king; all jurisdiction emanates from him. He has the right to dispense justice and to have it dispensed by his officials, to grant pardon, to bestow privileges and rewards, to establish offices, to confer nobility, to convoke and dismiss national assemblies whenever he judges it wise to do so, and to make peace and war and to call up the army.' (p. 28)

No doubt these are great prerogatives, but notice what the French constitution places on the other side of the balance.

---

line; he shows, in fact, an equal ignorance of languages, metaphysics, and history. [Rousseau accused Bodin of having confused *bourgeois* and *citoyen* because Bodin did not limit *citoyen* to the narrow Genevan usage.]

5. *Développement des principes fondamentaux de la monarchie française*, 1795. [This book was the work of a number of émigré magistrates of the parlements. It was written at Koblenz and Mannheim between the summer of 1791 and 1792 and submitted to the émigré princes in October 1792. Despite an adverse reaction from the princes, the authors published a revised version in 1795. Maistre erred in assuming that the book had Louis XVIII's approval; in fact, the king regarded it as a résumé of the claims of the parlements. The parlements' claim to a kind of veto power on royal legislative authority had been a matter of dispute between the crown and the high courts throughout the eighteenth century. The parlements are commonly blamed for obstructing the monarchy's reform efforts. But see William O. Doyle's 'The Parlements of France and the Breakdown of the Old Regime', *French Historical Studies*, Fall 1970, where the importance of the parlements as an obstacle to reform is discounted.]

'The king reigns only through the laws, and is powerless to act by mere whim.' (p. 364)

'There are laws that the kings themselves, as they have acknowledged in an expression that has become famous, are *happily powerless to violate*; these are the *laws of the realm*, in contrast to ordinary and nonconstitutional *royal* laws.' (pp. 29 and 30)

'Thus, for example, the succession to the crown is by the strict rule of male primogeniture. Marriages of princes of the blood made without royal consent are invalid. If the reigning dynasty dies out, it is the nation that gives itself a king, etc.' (pp. 263 ff.)

'The kings, as supreme legislators, have always spoken affirmatively in publishing their laws. Nevertheless there is also a consent of the people, although this consent is only an expression of the desire, the gratitude, and the acceptance of the nation.'[6] (p. 271)

'Three orders, three chambers, three deliberations— this is the way the nation is represented. The result of these deliberations, if unanimous, manifests the will of the Estates-General.' (p. 332)

'The laws of the realm can be made only by the general assembly of all the realm with the common consent of the three estates. The prince may not derogate from these laws, and if he dares meddle with them, what he does may be revoked by his successor.' (pp. 292 and 293)

6. If the intervention of the nation is examined closely, it will be found to be *less* than a colegislative power and *more* than simple consent. This is an example of the kind of thing that must be left in a certain obscurity and that cannot be submitted to human legislation. It is the *most divine part* of the constitution, if one may express it this way. It is often said that *it is only by making a law that we know where we stand*. Not always; there are *reserved cases*.

'The necessity of the consent of the nation in the establishment of taxes is an incontestable verity recognized by the kings.' (p. 302)

'The will of two orders cannot bind the third if the latter does not give its consent.' (p. 302)

'The consent of the Estates-General is necessary for the validity of any perpetual alienation of the domain, and the same surveillance is recommended to them to prevent any partial dismemberment of the domain.' (pp. 3 and 4)

'Justice is administered in the king's name by the magistrates who examine the laws to see if they are contrary to the fundamental laws.'

It is part of their duty to resist the misguided will of the sovereign. It was in reference to this principle that the famous Chancellor l'Hospital[7] told the Parlement of Paris in 1561:

'The magistrates must not allow themselves to be intimidated by the passing anger of a sovereign or by fear of disgrace, but must always remember their oath to obey the laws, which are the king's true commands.' (p. 345)

Louis XIV, halted by a double refusal by his parlement, desisted from an unconstitutional alienation. (p. 343)

Louis XIV solemnly recognized the right of free verification (p. 347) and ordered his magistrates *to disobey him under pain of disobedience* if he sent them orders contrary to the law (p. 345). This order was not a play on words: the king forbids obedience to the man; he has no greater enemy.

This superb monarch also ordered his magistrates to regard as null any letters patent bearing evocations or commissions for the judgement of civil or criminal cases, and *even to punish the bearers of these letters.* (p. 363)

7. [Michel de l'Hospital (1507–73) was chancellor of France from 1560 to 1568 during the French wars of religion.]

The magistrates can exclaim, *Happy land where servitude is unknown* (p. 361). And it is a priest distinguished by his piety and knowledge (Fleury)[8] who wrote in explaining public law in France, 'In France, every individual is free; there is no slavery; there is freedom of domicile, travel, commerce, marriage, choice of profession, acquisitions, disposition of goods, and inheritance.' (p. 362)

'The military power must not interfere with civil administration.' *Provincial governors have nothing to do with the army, and they may use armed force only against the enemies of the state, not against the citizen, who is submissive to the justice of the state.* (p. 364)

'The magistrates are irremovable, and these important offices can be vacated only by the death of the holder, voluntary resignation, or judicial judgement.' (p. 356)[9]

'The king, in cases concerning his own interests, pleads against his subjects in the courts. It has been known for him to be condemned to pay the tithe on the fruits of his gardens, etc.' (p. 367 ff.)

8. [C. F. Fleury (1640–1723), a celebrated Gallican prelate, wrote the twenty-volume *Histoire ecclésiastique*, which Maistre often cited.]

9. What is the point of declaiming so strongly against venality of office in the magistracy? If venality is seen as merely a means to hereditary tenure, the problem reduces itself to knowing whether, in a country such as France or such as France has been for two or three centuries, justice could be better administered than by hereditary magistrates. The question is very difficult to resolve; the enumeration of disadvantages is a deceptive argument. What is bad in a constitution, what may even destroy it, is nevertheless in fact a part of the constitution just as what is good. I recall a passage from Cicero: 'The tribunes of the plebs have too much power. Who can deny it? etc.' *De Legibus*, III, 10. [Cicero argues that every institution has its disadvantages as well as its advantages.]

If the French would look at themselves dispassionately and in good faith they would realize that this is enough, *perhaps more than enough* for a nation too noble to be enslaved and too impetuous to be free.

Does someone say that these fine laws were not observed? In this case, it was the fault of the French, and they have no hope of liberty; for when a people does not know how to take advantage of their own fundamental laws it is useless to look for others. It is a sign that they are not fit for liberty or that they are irremediably corrupt.

But to counter these sinister ideas, I will cite, on the excellence of the French constitution, a witness who is unexceptionable from every point of view—that great statesman and ardent republican, Machiavelli.

'There have been', he says, 'a great number of kings and very few good ones, I mean among absolute sovereigns. Among these, however, are not to be counted either the kings of Egypt in that ancient period when that country was governed by laws, or those of Sparta; neither those of France in modern times, for that country is more thoroughly regulated by laws than any other of which we have knowledge.'[10]

'The kingdom of France', he says elsewhere, 'is content and tranquil, because the king has bound himself by a number of laws that provide for the security of his people. He who organized that government[11] wanted the kings to dispose of the army and treasury at their own will, but to conform to the laws in all other matters.'[12]

Who would not be struck to see how this powerful mind understood the fundamental laws of the French monarchy three centuries ago?

10. *Discourses on Titus Livy*, Bk. I, ch. lviii.
11. I should like to know who it was.
12. *Discourses*, Bk. I, ch. xvi.

The French have been spoiled on this point by the English who have said, though without believing it themselves, that Frenchmen are slaves. Similarly the English told them that Shakespeare was better than Racine, and the French believed it. Even that honest judge, Blackstone, towards the end of his *Commentaries*, puts France on a par with Turkey. Here one would have to say with Montaigne, *One could not scoff enough at the impudence of this coupling.*

But when the English made their own revolution, at least in so far as they had one, did they suppress the king-ship or the House of Lords in order to achieve liberty? Not at all. Rather they activated their old constitution and took their declaration of rights from it.

There is not a Christian nation in Europe that is not by right *free* or *free enough*. There is not one that does not have, in the purest examples of its legislation, all the elements of the constitution that suits it. But it is especially necessary not to fall into the enormous error of believing that liberty is something absolute, something not subject to more or less. Jupiter casts the lots of nations, *more to one and less to the other*, and man has nothing to do with this distribution.

Another very deadly error is to be attached too rigidly to old ways. No doubt they must be respected, but what jurists call the *last state* must always be considered. Every free constitution is by its nature flexible, and flexible in the proportion to which it is free; it would be foolish to try to restore it to its rudiments without sacrificing something.[13]

Everything proves that the French sought to surpass human power, that these disorderly efforts are leading them into slavery, that they only needed to recognize what they

13. 'All human governments, particularly those of mixed frame, are in continual fluctuation.' Hume, *History of England, Charles I,* ch. i.

already possessed, and that if they are made for a greater degree of liberty than they enjoyed seven years ago (which is not at all clear) they have at hand in all the examples of their history and legislation everything they need to make them honoured and envied by all Europe.[14]

But if the French are made for monarchy and if it is only a question of establishing the monarchy on its true foundations, what error, what fatality, what disastrous prejudice could separate them from their legitimate king?

Hereditary succession in a monarchy is something so precious that every other consideration must give way before it. The greatest crime that a French royalist can commit is to see in Louis XVIII something other than his king or, by discussing the qualities of the man or his actions in an

---

14. A man whose person and opinion I equally respect (Mallet du Pan), who does not agree with me on the old French constitution, has taken the trouble of developing his ideas in an interesting letter for which I am most appreciative. Among other things he objects that 'the book of the French magistrates, cited in this chapter, would have been burned under the reign of Louis XIV or Louis XV as prejudicial to the fundamental laws of the monarchy and the rights of the monarch.' I believe it; so would Mr. Delolme's book (*On the English Constitution*) have been burned in London (perhaps with its author) under the reign of Henry VIII or his rude daughter.

When someone has taken a stand on great questions, with full knowledge of the cause, he rarely changes his mind. In the meantime, though I distrust my own prejudices as much as I must, I am sure of my own good faith. It should be noted that I cited no contemporary authorities in this chapter for fear that the most respectable might appear suspect. As to the magistrate authors of the *Développement des principes fondamentaux*, etc., if I used their work, it is just that I do not care to do what has been done, that the gentlemen cited certain documents, and this was precisely what I needed. [This note was added in the second edition. We do not have Mallet du Pan's letter.]

unfavourable way, to diminish the good will with which it is important to surround him. The Frenchman who would not blush to look into the past to find real or fancied mistakes would be very base and guilty. The accession to the throne is a new birth; one counts only from that instant.

If there is a commonplace in morals, it is that power and greatness corrupt men and that the best kings have been those who have been tried by adversity. So why do the French deprive themselves of the advantage of a prince formed by the terrible school of misfortune? How many reflections must the past six years provide him! How far removed from the intoxication of power! How ready he must be to undertake to rule gloriously and how inspired by worthy ambition!

Have Frenchmen not tested the blood of the Capets long enough? They know from a six-century-long experiment that this blood is good, so why change? The head of this great family has shown himself by his declaration to be loyal, generous, and profoundly inspired by religious truths; no one disputes his natural intelligence and excellent education. There was a time, perhaps, when an unlettered king was acceptable; but in this century, when we believe in books, an educated king is an advantage. What is more important is that he cannot be presumed to hold any of those exaggerated ideas capable of alarming the French. Who can forget that they were displeased with him at Koblenz? That episode is greatly in his favour. In his declaration he spoke of *liberty*, and if someone objects that the word was used guardedly, one can reply that a king must not speak the language of revolution. A solemn discourse addressed to his people must be distinguished by a certain sobriety of expression and ideas that has nothing in common with a private citizen's hasty opinions. When the king of France has stated *'that the French constitution sub-*

jects the laws to consecrated constitutional forms and the sovereign himself to the observation of the laws in order to guard the legislator's wisdom against seductive pitfalls and to defend the liberty of subjects against the abuses of authority,' he has said everything, since he has promised *liberty through the constitution*. The king must not speak like some Parisian tribune. If the king has discovered that it is a mistake to speak of liberty as something absolute, that liberty is on the contrary something susceptible to more or less, and that the art of the legislator is not to make a people free, but *free enough*, he has discovered a great truth, and he must be praised for his moderation rather than blamed. A famous Roman, giving liberty to a people long habituated to freedom, told them, *Libertate modice utendum*.[15] What would he have said to the French? Surely the king in speaking soberly of liberty was thinking less of his own interests than of those of the French.

'The constitution,' the king continues, 'prescribes the conditions for the establishment of taxes in order to assure the people that the taxes they pay are necessary for the welfare of the State.' Therefore, the king does not have the right to impose them arbitrarily, and this avowal alone excludes despotism.

'It confides the registration of laws to the highest body of magistrates so that they may watch over their execution and so that they may enlighten the monarch's judgement if he has erred.' There you have registration of laws in the hands of the high magistracy; there you have the consecration of the right of remonstrance. And whenever a body of hereditary, or at least irremovable, magistrates has the constitutional right to warn the monarch, to elucidate his judgement, and to complain of abuses, there is no despotism.

15. Titus Livy, XXXIV, 49. [They should use their liberty with discretion.]

'It places the fundamental laws under the safeguard of the king and the three orders so as to prevent revolution, the greatest calamity that can befall a people.'

Thus there is a constitution, since the constitution is only the collection of fundamental laws, and the king cannot touch these laws. If he tried to, the three orders would have a *veto* over him, as each of the orders has over the other two.

And surely it would be mistaken to accuse the king of having spoken too vaguely, for this vagueness is precisely the proof of the highest wisdom. The king would have acted very imprudently if he had posed bounds that would have prevented him from manoeuvring; it was an inspiration to reserve a certain latitude of execution for himself. Someday the French will agree, and admit that the king promised everything that he could have promised.

Did Charles I find himself better off for having adhered to the propositions of the Scots? He was told, as Louis XVIII has been told, 'It is necessary to adapt to the times, to be flexible. *It is folly to sacrifice a crown to save the hierarchy.*' He believed it, and acted very badly. The king of France is wiser. How can the French be so obstinate as not to render him justice?

If this prince had been so foolish as to propose a new constitution to the French, then they could have accused him of indulging in perfidious vagueness, for in so doing he would have said nothing. If he had proposed a work of his own creation, there would only have been an outcry against him, and the outcry would have been well founded. By what right, in effect, could he command obedience once he abandoned the old laws? Is not arbitrariness a common domain to which everyone has equal right? There is not a young man in France who would not point out the faults in a new constitution and propose amendments. Look at the matter carefully and you will see that as soon as the king had abandoned the old constitution, he would have had only one thing left to say: 'I will do whatever you wish.' Translated into plain French, this is the indecent and absurd proposition to which the king's beautiful discourse would have been reduced. Does it really show serious thought to blame the king for not having offered the French a new revolution? Since the insurrections which began his family's dreadful misfortunes he has seen three constitutions accepted, sworn to, and solemnly consecrated. The first two lasted no time at all, and the third exists in name only. Should the king have offered his subjects five or six and let them take their choice? Certainly the first three cost enough that no sensible man would be advised to suggest another. But such a proposal, which would be folly on the part of a private citizen, would be foolish and criminal on the king's part.

No matter what he did, the king could not have made everyone happy. There would have been objections if he had published no declaration, there were objections to the one he published, and there would have been objections to any other. In a doubtful situation, he did well to stand on principle, offending only passion and prejudice in saying that *the French constitution would be his ark of the covenant.* If Frenchmen would examine this declaration dispassionately, I would be most surprised if they did not find there good reasons for respecting the king. In the terrible circumstances in which he found himself, nothing could have been more attractive than the temptation to compromise on principle in order to reconquer the throne. So many people said and believed that the king was losing by his obstinate attachment to old ideas! It would have appeared so natural to listen to proposals of accommodation! Above all, it would have been so easy to accede to these proposals with the mental reservation to regain the old prerogative, not dishonestly, but relying on the force of things, that it took a great deal of frankness, nobility, and courage to tell Frenchmen, 'I cannot make you happy; I can, I must, reign only constitutionally: I will not meddle with the Lord's ark; I am waiting for you to come back to your senses; I am waiting until you have grasped this truth that is so simple and so self-evident and that you still obstinately reject, which is *that with the same constitution* I can give you a totally different regime.'

The king showed his wisdom by telling the French that *their old and sensible constitution was for him a sacred ark and that he was forbidden to alter it lightly*. However, he added that *he wanted to restore all its purity and vigour, which time had corrupted and weakened*. Once again, these are inspired words, for they clearly separate what pertains to human power from what belongs to God. There is not a single phrase in this too-unappreciated document that should not recommend the king to the French.

It is hoped that this impetuous nation, which knows how to return to the truth only after having exhausted error, will finally want to perceive a very palpable truth; this is that it is the dupe and victim of a small number of men who place themselves between the nation and its legitimate sovereign, from whom only benefits can be expected. Put things at their worst: *the king will allow the hand of justice to fall on some parricides; he will punish by humiliation some nobles who have displeased him*. Eh! What does this matter to you, good workman, industrious artisan, peaceable citizen, whoever you may be, to whom heaven has given obscurity and happiness? Remember that you, with your fellows, form almost the whole nation and that the entire people suffers all the evils of anarchy because a handful of scoundrels has made the nation afraid of the king whom they fear.

If Frenchmen continue to reject their king they will be

allowing a uniquely auspicious occasion to elude them, and they will expose themselves to rule by force instead of crowning their legitimate sovereign themselves. How the king would cherish them and by what efforts of zeal and love would he seek to repay their fidelity! The national will would always be before his eyes to inspire the great enterprise and the hard work that the regeneration of France demands of this leader, and every minute of his life would be consecrated to the happiness of Frenchmen.

But if they obstinately reject their king, do they know what their lot will be? Hardship has by now matured the French enough for them to understand a hard truth: the fact is that the neutral witness observing them in the midst of their frantic liberty is often tempted to cry out, like Tiberius, *O hominus ad servitutem natus!*[16] There are, as we know, several kinds of courage, and Frenchmen certainly do not possess them all. Intrepid in the face of the enemy they are less than brave before even the most unjust authority. Nothing equals the patience of this people that calls itself *free*. In five years they have been made to accept three constitutions and the revolutionary government. Tyrants succeeded one another and the people always obeyed. Not a single one of their efforts to extricate themselves from their predicament succeeded. Their masters have gone so far as to crush them by mocking them. They told the people, 'You believe that you do not want this law, but you can be sure that you do. If you dare refuse it, we will shoot you down with grapeshot to punish you for not wanting what you want.' And they did it.[17]

The French nation is no longer under Robespierre's

16. [Oh men born to servitude.]

17. [An allusion to the Vendémiaire uprising of 5 October 1795, which young General Bonaparte put down with grapeshot.]

frightful yoke, but this makes no difference. They may well congratulate themselves for having escaped this tyranny, but they have nothing to boast about. I am not sure that their time of servitude was more shameful than that of their emancipation. The history of the ninth of Thermidor is short: *a few scoundrels killed a few scoundrels.* If it had not been for this family quarrel Frenchmen would still be groaning under the rule of the Committee of Public Safety.

And who knows what still awaits them? They have given such proof of their patience that there is no kind of degradation that they cannot expect. I suggest this is a great lesson, not only for the French people, who more than any other people in the world will always accept their masters and never choose them, but for the small number of good Frenchmen made influential by circumstances, to neglect nothing to save the nation from these degrading fluctuations by delivering it into the hands of the king. No doubt he is human, but do they expect to be governed by an angel? He is human, but today we are sure that he knows this, and this is a great deal. If the wish of Frenchmen were to place him on his father's throne, he would embrace his nation, and the nation would find in him everything it desired: goodness, justice, love, gratitude, and incontestable talents matured in the hard school of adversity.[18]

The French have appeared to pay little attention to the words of peace that he has addressed to them. They have not praised his declaration, they have even criticized it and probably they have forgotten it; but some day they will render him justice, some day posterity will refer to this statement as a model of royal wisdom, frankness, and style.

The duty of every good Frenchman at this moment is to work untiringly to direct public opinion in favour of the

18. I will return to the interesting problem of amnesty in Chapter 10.

king and to present his every act in a favourable light. Royalists must examine their consciences severely on this point and permit themselves no illusions. I am not a Frenchman, I know nothing of their intrigues; I am not personally involved with these people. But supposing a French royalist said to me, 'I am ready to spill my blood for the king; however, without derogating from the loyalty I owe him, I cannot help but blame him, etc.,' I would tell him what his conscience would already be shouting: 'You are lying to the world and to yourself; if you were capable of sacrificing your life for the king, you could sacrifice your prejudices for him. Moreover, he does not need your life, he needs rather your prudence, your measured zeal, your passive devotion, even (to cover all possibilities) your indulgence. Keep your life, which he does not need at the moment, and give him those services he does need. Do you think those who make the newspapers are the most heroic? On the contrary, the most obscure can be the most efficacious and the most sublime. It is not your pride that is at stake here; satisfy your conscience and Him who gave you a conscience.'

Just as threads which can be broken by a child at play can nevertheless be joined to form a cable capable of supporting the anchor of a great vessel, so a number of insignificant criticisms can create a formidable force. To combat these prejudices that somehow spring up and for some reason continue to flourish would be to serve the king well. Has not the king been reproached for inaction by men who should know better! Have not others haughtily compared him to Henry IV, observing that that great prince was quite able to find other means of regaining his throne than intrigues and declamations? But if one is going to be funny, why not reproach the king for not having conquered Germany and Italy as Charlemagne did and for not living there in great style while waiting for the French to listen to reason?

As to the more or less numerous party that is raising great outcries against the monarchy and monarch, it is animated by more than mere hate. It is worth analysing what is involved.

There is not an intelligent man in France who is not more or less disgusted with himself. Every heart is burdened by the nation's ignominy (for never was a people despised by more miserable masters). So they need to comfort themselves, and good citizens do it in their own way. But the vile and corrupt man, for whom all elevated ideas are foreign, revenges himself for his past and present abjection by contemplating the spectacle of humiliated greatness with the ineffable delight of the lowly. To raise himself in his own eyes, he looks down on the king of France, and he is assured of his own stature by comparing himself to this overturned colossus. Unconsciously, by a trick of his disordered imagination, he comes to regard this great collapse as his own work; he invests himself with all the power of the republic; he reproaches the king; he haughtily calls him a *so-called Louis XVIII*; and blasting the monarchy in furious pamphlets, like one of La Fontaine's heroes, he thinks himself a *thunderbolt of war* if he manages to frighten a few *Chouans*.[19]

We must also take account of the fear that howls against the king, the fear that his return will mean one more rifle shot.

People of France, do not allow yourselves to be seduced by the sophisms of private interest, vanity, or cowardice. Do not listen to the reasoners; there has been too much

19. [Chouans were bands of rebellious peasants, royalists, and outlaws who troubled the peace of Brittany and other areas in the west of France during the period of the Directory.]

reasoning in France, and reasoning has banished reason. Put aside your fears and reservations, and trust the infallible instinct of your conscience. Do you want to redeem yourselves in your own eyes? Do you want to acquire the right of self-esteem? Do you want to accomplish a sovereign act? . . . Recall your sovereign.

I am a perfect stranger to France, which I have never seen, and I expect nothing from her king, whom I shall never know. So if I commit some errors, Frenchmen can at least read them calmly as entirely disinterested errors.

But what are we, weak and blind human beings! And what is that flickering light we call *Reason*? When we have calculated all the probabilities, questioned history, satisfied every doubt and special interest, we may still embrace only a deceptive shadow rather than the truth. What decree has He pronounced on the king, on his dynasty, on his family, on France, and on Europe? Where and when will the troubles end, and by how many misfortunes must we purchase our tranquillity? Is it to destroy that He has overthrown, or are our hardships to last forever? Alas! A dark cloud hides the future and no eye can penetrate its shadows. Nevertheless, everything announces that the present situation in France cannot last and that invincible nature must restore the monarchy. So whether our wishes are accomplished or whether inexorable Providence has decided otherwise, it is curious and even useful to study how these great changes occur and what role the multitude might play in an event whose date appears doubtful, never losing sight of history and the nature of man.

IX

How Will the Counter-Revolution Happen If It Comes?

In theorizing about the counter-revolution, men have too often assumed that this counter-revolution should and could be solely the result of popular deliberation.[1] 'The people fear,' they say, 'the people want, the people will never consent, it does not suit the people, etc.' What a pity! The people count for nothing in revolutions, or at most count only as a passive instrument. Four or five persons, perhaps, will give France a king. Letters from Paris will announce to the provinces that France has a king, and the provinces will cry 'Long live the king.' Even in Paris, all but a twentieth of the inhabitants, perhaps, will learn some

---

1. [Joseph de Maistre was quite proud of this chapter. After the Restoration he asked a friend to reread his 'Considérations sur la France, where, by signal good fortune, everything was prophetic, down to the names of two of the cities that were the first to recognize the king, Lyons and Bordeaux'. Letter to Count J. Potocki, 28 October 1814, Oeuvres, 12: 461.]

morning that they have a king. 'Is it possible?' they will exclaim. 'Isn't this a strange turn of events? Does anyone know by what gate he will be entering? Perhaps it would be wise to rent windows in advance, for there will be crushing crowds.' If the monarchy is restored, the people will no more decree its restoration than they decreed its destruction or the establishment of the revolutionary government.

I beg that my reflections be considered carefully, and I recommend them particularly to those who believe revolution to be impossible because there are too many Frenchmen attached to the Republic and because a change would cause suffering for too many. *Scilicet is superis labor est!*[2] Whether or not the Republic has the support of the majority is certainly open to dispute, but whether it does or not makes no difference at all. Enthusiasm and fanaticism are not lasting phenomena. Human nature soon tires of this kind of ecstasy. So even supposing that a people, and the French people in particular, may want something for a long time, it is still certain that they will not want it passionately for a long time. On the contrary, the peak of the fever having subsided, great outbursts of enthusiasm are always followed by despondency, apathy, and indifference. This is precisely the situation in France at the moment, where nothing is desired passionately except repose. Even if we supposed that the majority in France supported the Republic (which is indubitably false), what of it? When the king appears, it is certain that heads will not be counted and that no one will stir: first, because even those who prefer the Republic to the monarchy prefer their repose to the Republic, and second, because those opposed to the crown will be unable to unite.

In politics as in mechanics, theories fail if they do not

2. Vergil, *Aeneid*, IV, 379. [Truly, this is work for gods.]

take into consideration the different qualities of the materials that make up the machines. At first glance, for example, it appears true that *the prior consent of the French is necessary for the restoration of the monarchy*. Yet nothing is more false. Let us leave theory and take a look at the facts.

A courier arrives in Bordeaux, Nantes, Lyons, etc., carrying the news that the king's authority has been acknowledged in Paris, that such-and-such faction (which may or may not be named) has seized power and declared that it is exercising authority in the king's name, that a courier has been dispatched to the sovereign, who is expected forthwith, and that the white cockade is being displayed everywhere. Rumour takes the news and adds a thousand impressive details. What will people do? To give the Republic every chance, I grant it a majority and even a corps of republican troops. At first, perhaps, these troops will display a rebellious attitude; but they will want to eat, and they will soon begin to detach themselves from the regime that no longer pays them. Every officer, feeling quite clearly the lack of recognition accorded him by the republican regime no matter what he is told, also sees clearly that the first to cry 'Long live the king' will become a great hero. His self-esteem sketches the colourful and seductive image of a splendidly decorated general in the armies of His Most Christian Majesty haughtily reviewing those same men who not long since would have had him up before the municipal court. These ideas are so simple and so natural that they can escape no one. Every officer senses what is happening, and it follows that they suspect one another. Fear and distrust produce indecision and coolness. The soldier, no longer spurred on by his officer, becomes even more discouraged: the disciplinary bond receives an inexplicable blow, a magic blow that suddenly snaps it. One man looks towards the royal paymaster who is coming, another takes advantage of the opportunity to rejoin his family. They no longer command or obey; they no longer act together.

Among the citizens it is another story. They are coming and going, disputing and questioning one another. Everyone fears those whom he would need to trust; doubts consume hours when minutes are decisive. Everywhere prudence inhibits audacity; the old lack determination, and the young lack counsel. On one side there are terrible risks, on the other certain amnesty and probable favours. In addition, where are the means to resist? And where are the leaders who can be trusted? There is no danger in repose, and the least action may prove an unpardonable mistake. So one must wait. They wait, but the next day they receive news that such-and-such city has opened its gates. More reason not to act precipitously. It is soon learned that the news was false, but two other cities, believing it true, have given the example. Accepting the news as true, they have just submitted and decisively influenced the first, which had not thought of yielding. The governor of the place has presented the king with the keys of *his good city of* ————. He is the first officer who has had the honour of receiving the king in a citadel of his realm. The king made him a marshal of France on the spot. *Innumerable fleur-de-lis* cover him with immortal honour, his name will be renowned forever in France. Every minute the royalist movement is being reinforced; soon it becomes irresistible. 'Long live the king,' cry the loving and the loyal, beside themselves with joy. 'Long live the king,' responds the republican hypocrite in dire terror. What does it matter? There is only one cry. And the king is crowned.

Citizens! This is how counter-revolutions are made. God warns us that He has reserved to Himself the establishment of sovereignties by never confiding to the masses the choice of their masters. In these great moments that decide the fate of empires, He employs them only as a passive instrument. Never do they get what they want; they always accept, they never choose. One may even notice that it is an affectation of Providence, if I may be permitted the expression, that the efforts of a people to obtain a goal are precisely the means that Providence employs to keep them from it. Thus the Roman people gave themselves masters while believing they were opposing the aristocracy by following Caesar. This is the image of all popular insurrections. In the French Revolution the people have continually been enslaved, outraged, ruined, and mutilated by all parties, and the parties in their turn, working one against the other, have continually drifted, despite all their efforts, toward breakup at length on the rocks awaiting them.

If one wants to know the probable result of the French Revolution, it suffices to examine that which united all parties. They have all wanted the debasement, even the destruction, of the universal Church and the monarchy, *from which it follows* that all their efforts will culminate in the glorification of Christianity and the monarchy.

All men who have written on or reflected about history have admired this secret force that makes sport of human plans. One such man was that great captain of antiquity who honoured this force as an intelligent and free power and who undertook nothing without recommending himself to it.[3]

But it is especially in the establishment and overthrow of sovereignties that the action of Providence shows itself in the most striking way. Not only do the people as a whole

3. 'For he believed that nothing in human affairs happened without the design of the gods; and for that reason he had established in his house a shrine of fortune, which he venerated most religiously.' Cornelius Nepos, *Life of Timoleon*, ch. iv.

participate in these great movements only like wood and rope used by a workman, but even their leaders are only such to untrained eyes: in fact, they are ruled just as much as they rule the people. These men who, taken together, seem to be the tyrants of the multitude are themselves tyrannized by two or three men, who are tyrannized by one. And if this single individual could and wanted to reveal his secret, you would see that he does not know himself how he gained power, that his influence is a greater mystery to himself than to others, and that circumstances which he could neither foresee nor affect have done everything for him and without him.

Who could have told the proud Henry VI that a servant girl would snatch from him the sceptre of France?[4] The noisome explanations that have been given of this great event have not stripped it of its marvels; and although it has been dishonoured twice, first by the absence, and then by the prostitution, of talent,[5] it nevertheless remains the sole subject in French history worthy of an epic muse.

Do you believe that *these arms will be shortened*, which once used so feeble an instrument, that the Supreme Commander of Empires will take the advice of the French to give them a king? No, He will again choose, as He has always done, the *weakest to confound the strongest*. He has no need of foreign armies, He has no need of the *coalition*, and just as He has preserved the integrity of France despite the counsels and power of so many princes, *who are before His eyes as if they were not*, when the time comes, He will restore the French monarchy despite its enemies. He will

4. [Henry VI of England (1422–61) had been proclaimed king of France at the death of Charles VI, but Joan of Arc's intervention led to the coronation and recognition of Charles VII as king.]

5. [Chapelain's *La Pucelle* (1656) and Voltaire's *La Pucelle* (1755).]

chase out these noisy insects *pulveris exigui jactu:*[6] the king will come, he will see, he will conquer.

Then you will be astonished by the profound nullity of these men who appeared so powerful. Today it belongs to the wise to predict this judgement and to be sure, before experience proves it, that the rulers of France possess only an artificial and transitory power, of which the very excess proves the nothingness, 'that their stock was neither planted, nor sown, nor rooted in the earth, and that a whirlwind shall take them away like straw'.[7]

So it is fruitless for so many writers to insist on the difficulties in the way of the restoration of the monarchy; it is fruitless for them to frighten the French with the consequences of a counter-revolution. And when they conclude that the French, dreading these difficulties, will never allow the restoration of the monarchy, they argue very badly, for the French will not be deliberating. Perhaps they will receive a king from the hand of a maid.

No nation can give itself a government; at most, when such-and-such a right exists in its constitution,[8] and this right is unrecognized or suppressed, certain men, aided by circumstances, may be able to push aside the obstacles and gain acknowledgement of the people's rights. Human power extends no further.

For the rest, although Providence is not the least embarrassed by what it might cost the French to have a king, it is nevertheless very important to observe that writers who frighten the French with the misfortunes that the restoration of the monarchy might entail are certainly in error or bad faith.

6. Vergil, *Georgics*, IV, 87. [Tossing a little dust.]
7. Isaias, 40:24.
8. I mean its *natural* constitution, for its *written* constitution is only paper.

X

On the Supposed Dangers of a Counter-Revolution

General Considerations

It is common fallacy nowadays to insist on the danger of counter-revolution in order to show that we should not return to the monarchy. A great number of works designed to persuade the French to hold fast to the Republic are only developments of this idea. The authors of these works stress the evils inseparable from revolutions; then, observing that the monarchy cannot be restored in France without a new revolution, they conclude from this that the Republic must be maintained. This stupendous fallacy, whether it arises from fear or from the desire to deceive, deserves to be carefully discussed.

Almost all errors spring from the misuse of words. It has become customary to give the name *counter-revolution* to any movement aimed at stopping the Revolution. Because such a movement must work against the Revolution, some would conclude that it would be simply a reverse revolution. But would it be argued, for example, that the return from sickness to health must be as painful as the passage from health to sickness? Or that because the monarchy was overthrown by monstrous men that it must be restored by the same type? Ah, if those who peddle this fallacy would only be honest with themselves! They know full well that the friends of religion and monarchy are incapable of the excesses with which their enemies have besmirched themselves. They know full well, even taking things at their worst, taking full account of human weaknesses, that the oppressed party is a thousand times more virtuous than their oppressors. They know full well that the first group knows not how to defend or revenge itself and is often enough openly mocked on this account.

In order to effect the French Revolution, it was necessary to overthrow religion, outrage morality, violate every propriety, and commit every crime. This diabolical work required the employment of such a number of vicious men that perhaps never before had so many vices acted together to accomplish any evil whatsoever. In contrast, to restore order the king will call on all the virtues; no doubt he will wish to do this, but by the very nature of things he will be forced to do so. His most pressing interest will be to unite justice and mercy; honourable men will come of themselves to take up positions in posts where they can be of use, and religion, lending its authority to politics, will give the strength that can be drawn only from this august sister.

I have no doubt that many men will ask to be shown the bases of these magnificent hopes; but can we believe that the political world operates by chance, that it is not organized, directed, and animated by the same wisdom that is revealed in the physical world? The guilty hands that overthrow a state necessarily inflict grievous wounds, for no free agent can thwart the plans of the Creator without incurring in the sphere of his activity evils proportionate to the extent of the crime. This law pertains more to the goodness of the Supreme Being than to his justice.

But when man works to restore order he associates himself with the author of order; he is favoured by *nature*, that is to say, by the ensemble of secondary forces that are the agents of the Divinity. His action partakes of the divine; it becomes both gentle and imperious, forcing nothing yet not resisted by anything. His arrangements restore health. As he acts, he calms disquiet and the painful agitation that is the effect and symptom of disorder. In the same way, the hands of a skilful surgeon bring the cessation of pain that proves the dislocated joint has been put right.

Frenchmen, it was to the noise of hellish songs, the blasphemy of atheism, the cries of death, and the prolonged moans of slaughtered innocence, it was by the light of flames, on the debris of throne and altar, watered by the blood of the best of kings and an innumerable host of other victims, it was by the contempt of morality and the established faith, it was in the midst of very crime that your seducers and your tyrants founded what they call *your liberty*.

It will be in the name of the VERY GOOD AND VERY GREAT GOD, in the train of men whom He loves and inspires, and under the influence of His creative power that you will return to your old constitution and that a king will give you the only thing that you ought wisely to desire—*liberty through the monarchy*.

What deplorable blindness makes you persist in fighting painfully against the power that renders vain all your efforts in order to warn you of its presence? You are powerless only because you have dared to separate yourself from it and even to oppose it. The moment you act in concert with it you will participate in some way in its nature;

every obstacle will be levelled before you, and you will laugh at the childish fears that are disturbing you at present. All parts of the political machine have a natural tendency toward the place assigned to them, and this tendency will favour all the king's efforts; and order being the natural element of man, you will find there the happiness that you have vainly sought in disorder. The Revolution made you suffer because it was the work of every vice, and the vices are very justly man's executioners. For the opposite reason, the return of the monarchy, far from producing the evils that you fear for the future, will arrest those that devour you today. All your efforts will be positive; you will destroy only destruction.

Rid yourself for once of these distressing doctrines that have dishonoured our century and ruined France. You have already learned to know the preachers of these fatal dogmas for what they are, but the impression they have made on you has not been effaced. In all your plans for creation and restoration, you forget only God. They have separated you from Him; it is only by an effort of reasoning that you raise your thoughts to the inexhaustible source of all existence. You want to see only man—his actions so weak, so dependent, so circumscribed, his will so corrupt, so irresolute—and the existence of a superior cause is only a theory for you. Nevertheless, it presses in on you and surrounds you; you feel it, and the entire universe announces it to you. When you are told that without it you have power only to destroy, this is no vain theory you are sold, this is a practical truth founded on the experience of every age and on the knowledge of human nature. Look at history and you will not see any institution of any strength or duration that does not rest on a divine idea. It does not matter what kind of idea, for there is no entirely false religious system. So talk no more of difficulties and the evils that alarm you as the consequence of what you call counter-revolution. All the evils that you have suffered come from yourselves. Why should you not have been wounded by the ruins of the edifice that you have brought down upon yourselves? Reconstruction is another order of things; you have only to reenter the way that can take you there. You will never create anything following the path of nothingness.

Oh, these deceitful or cowardly writers who are guilty of terrifying people with this vain bugbear they call counter-revolution! These writers who agree that the Revolution was a frightful scourge, but who still maintain that it is impossible to turn back. Do they say that the evils of the Revolution are over and the French have completed their journey? The people were so crushed and intimidated by Robespierre's reign that any state of affairs where there is no longer uninterrupted killing seems happy and bearable. During the height of the Terror, foreigners noticed that all the letters from France that recounted the ghastly scenes of this cruel period ended with the remark 'At the moment, things are quiet.' Which is to say, 'The executioners are resting, they are regaining their strength, everything goes well while we wait.' The feeling has survived the infernal regime that created it. Petrified by the terror and discouraged by the policy errors of foreign powers, the Frenchman has shut himself up in an egoism that prevents him from seeing any more than himself and his present time and place. Assassinations are occurring in a hundred places in France; it does not matter, he is not being pillaged or massacred. If crime is committed on his street or in his neighbour's house, again what does it matter? It has already happened, *now it is quiet*. He will double his locks and not think about it. In a word, every Frenchman is happy enough as long as he is not being killed.

Nevertheless the laws are unenforced and the government recognizes its impotence to execute them. The most infamous crimes are increasingly common in all parts of the country; the revolutionary demon is proudly raising its head again. The constitution is no more than a spider web, and the regime permits itself horrible outrages. Marriage has become legal prostitution; there is no more paternal authority, no more fear of crime, no more shelter for the indigent. Hideous suicides proclaim to the government the despair of the unfortunates who accuse it. People are being demoralized in the most frightening way; the absence of religion joined to the total absence of public education is preparing for France a generation the very idea of which makes one shudder.

Cowardly optimists! This is the order of things that you are afraid to see changed! Shake off your miserable lethargy! Instead of showing people imaginary woes that might result from a change, use your talents to make them desire the gentle and health-giving agitation that will bring the king back to his throne and restore order in France.

Show us, too-busy men, show us these terrible misfortunes that so menace you as to disgust you with the monarchy. Do you not see that your republican institutions have no roots, that they are simply *sitting* on your soil in contrast to their predecessors, which were *planted* there? It took an axe to fell the latter; a breath will sweep away the other and leave not a trace. Surely it is not all the same thing to take away the hereditary rank of a president of a parlement, which rank was his property, as it is to dismiss a temporary judge without rank. The Revolution caused so much suffering because it destroyed so much, because it suddenly and harshly violated every kind of propriety, prejudice, and custom. Because every plebeian tyranny is by its very nature impetuous, insulting, and ruthless, that which accomplished the French Revolution had to push these characteristics to excess. The world has never seen a baser or more absolute tyranny.

Men are most sensitive to opinion; wounded here, they raise the greatest fuss. This is what made the Revolution so painful, because it trampled under foot all nobility of opinion. Now even if the restoration of the monarchy caused the same real privations for the same number of men, there would still be an immense difference in that it would not destroy any dignity, for there is no dignity in France at the moment for the same reason that there is no sovereignty.

But even if we consider only the physical privations, the difference would be no less striking. The usurper slew the innocent; the king will pardon the guilty. The one confiscated legitimate property; the other will be hesitant to disturb illegitimate property. The one took for its motto *Diruit, aedificat, mutat quodrata rotundis.*[1] After seven years of trying, it still cannot organize a primary school or a country festival; even its partisans mock its laws, its officials, its institutions, its celebrations, and even its costumes. The other, building on a true foundation, will not be groping; an unseen force will preside at its acts; it will disturb only to restore. Moreover, all orderly action torments only evil.

Again, it is a great error to imagine that the people have something to lose in the restoration of the monarchy, for the only thing the people won from the general upheaval was an idea: *they have equal right to all positions*, it is said. What is involved? It is a question of knowing what these positions are worth. These positions, which were so ostentatiously offered the people as a great conquest, are in fact

1. Horace, *Ep.* I, 100. [Pulling down, building up, and changing square to round.]

worth nothing before the tribunal of public opinion. Even the military profession, more honoured in France than any other, has lost its lustre; it is no longer highly regarded, and peace will lower its prestige even more. They threaten the military with the restoration of the monarchy, and yet none have more to gain. There is nothing so evident as the necessity that will require the king to maintain them at their posts. And dependence on them will sooner or later change this political necessity into a necessity of affection, respect, and recognition. Through an extraordinary combination of circumstances, there is nothing about the military that could shock the most royalist opinion. None have a right to sneer at them, since they fought only for France. So there is no prejudicial barrier between them and the king capable of hampering mutual respect. He is a Frenchman above all. They should recall James II during the battle of the Hogue[2] applauding from the shore the valour of the Englishmen who had managed to dethrone him. Can they doubt that the king is proud of their valour and that he regards them in his heart as the defenders of the integrity of his kingdom? Has he not publicly applauded this valour while regretting (it must be noted) *that it was not displayed for a better cause*? Has he not congratulated the brave men of Condé's army *for having defeated the hatreds that the deepest artifice has laboured so long to nourish*?[3] The French military, after their victories, have only one need: this is that legitimate sovereignty comes to legitimize their status, for now they are feared and despised. The most complete unconcern is the reward of their labours, and their fellow citizens are of all people the most indifferent

2. [The English and Dutch fleets defeated the French fleet off La Hogue in 1692.]

3. Letter from the king to the prince de Condé of 3 January 1797, printed in all the newspapers.

to the army's triumph. They often go so far as to detest these victories that nourish the warlike temper of their masters. The restoration of the monarchy will immediately restore the military to a high place in public opinion; talents will be on the way to winning a real dignity, an ever-increasing lustre that will always be the warrior's due and that they will pass on to their children. This pure glory, this quiet splendour, will be worth more than the honourable mentions and the ostracism of forgetfulness that has succeeded the scaffold.

If the question is looked at from the most general point of view, it will be found that monarchy is, without contradiction, the form of government that gives the most distinction to the greatest number of persons. Sovereignty in this kind of government possesses enough brilliance to be able to share a part of it, with the necessary gradations, with a crowd of its more or less distinguished agents. In a republic, sovereignty is not tangible, as it is in a monarchy; it is a purely moral concept, and its greatness is incommunicable. In addition, in republics public offices are nothing outside the capital city, and moreover, they are nothing except insofar as they are occupied by members of government. Then it is the man who honours the office, not the office that honours the man, so that the man is honoured not as an agent but as a *portion* of sovereignty.

One can see that in countries obeying republican governments public office (if those reserved to the members of the sovereign are excluded) raises men very little in the eyes of their fellow citizens and has practically no significance in public opinion. This is because a republic is, by its nature, the government that gives the most rights to the very small number of men who are called the *sovereign* and that takes away the most from all the others, who are called *subjects*.

The nearer a republic approaches a pure democracy, the more striking this observation becomes. Just recall the innumerable offices (even omitting all the useless ones) that the old government of France offered to universal ambition. The secular clergy, the regular clergy, the sword, the robe, finance, administration, etc. were all doors open to every kind of talent and ambition! What incalculable gradations of personal distinction! In this infinite number of places none was beyond the legitimate aspirations of the ordinary citizen;[4] there were even a great number that were valuable properties, that really made the possessor a *notable*, and that belonged exclusively to the Third Estate.

The highest positions were more difficult for the ordinary citizen to obtain, but this is quite reasonable. There is too much movement in a state and not enough subordination when *everyone* can aspire to *everything*. Order requires that, in general, offices be graded like the condition of citizens, and that the barriers that separate the different classes be let down only to talents, and sometimes simply to patronage. In this way, there is emulation without humiliation and movement without destruction; the distinction attached to an office is the product, as the word implies, of the greater or lesser difficulty of obtaining it.

To object that these distinctions are bad is to change the question. But I would say, 'If your offices do not elevate those possessing them, do not boast of giving them to everyone, for you are not giving them anything. If, on the contrary, offices do and must mean distinctions, I repeat that no honest man can deny that monarchy is the government that through offices alone, and independently of the

4. The famous law that excluded the Third Estate from military service could not be enforced; it was simply a ministerial blunder that passion spoke of as a fundamental law.

nobility, *distinguishes* the greatest number of men from their fellow citizens.'

Moreover, one must not be the dupe of that ideal equality that is only a matter of words. The soldier who has the privilege of talking to his officer in a grossly familiar tone is not by that his equal. An aristocracy of office that could not at first be perceived in the general confusion is beginning to emerge; even the nobility is regaining its indestructible influence. The army and the navy are already commanded, in part, by gentlemen or by the students that the old regime had ennobled by admitting to a noble profession. Indeed, these men won the republic its greatest successes. If the perhaps unfortunate delicacy of the French nobility had not led them to leave France, they would be in command everywhere. It is common enough to hear it said *that if the nobility had been willing they would have been given all the offices.* Certainly, at the moment I write (4 January 1797), the Republic would very much like to have its vessels manned by the nobles whom it massacred at Quiberon.[5]

So the people, or the mass of citizens, have nothing to lose; on the contrary, they have everything to gain with the restoration of the monarchy, which will bring back a multitude of real, lucrative, and even hereditary distinctions in place of the insecure and undignified jobs that the Republic provides. I do not have to insist on the financial

5. [With the failure of the disastrous Quiberon expedition of 1795, some six thousand men, including about one thousand émigrés, were taken prisoner by General Hoche. The émigrés were shot. The representative reporting the list of those executed to the Committee of Public Safety wrote, 'The entire prerevolutionary navy landed at Quiberon.' Another contemporary commented, 'Hoche won . . . but he killed the French navy.' See E. Gabory, 'Le supplice des émigrés pris à Quiberon', *Revue des Deux Mondes*, 15 July 1930.]

compensation attached to offices, since it is notorious that the Republic pays poorly or not at all. It has produced only scandalous fortunes; only vice is enriched in its service.

I will conclude this section with some observations that (it seems to me) prove clearly that the danger that counter-revolution is said to involve is to be found precisely in delaying this great change.

The Bourbon family cannot be touched by the republican leaders; it exists, its rights are apparent, and its silence speaks louder perhaps than any manifesto.

It is perfectly obvious that the French Republic, even though it seems to have softened its maxims, can have no real allies. By its nature, it is the enemy of every government; it tends to destroy them all, so that all have an interest in destroying it. Politics may no doubt give allies to the Republic, but these alliances are unnatural, or if you prefer, *France* has allies but the French *republic* has none.[6]

Friends and enemies will always agree to give France a king. The success of the English Revolution of the last century is often cited—but what a difference! The monarchy was not overthrown in England. The monarch alone disappeared to make room for another. The very blood of the Stuarts was on the throne, and it was this that gave the new king his claim. This king had the advantage of being a strong prince with all the strength of his House and his family relationships. Moreover, the English government posed no dangers to other governments; it was a monarchy,

6.　　We know it: this licence we poets claim
　　　　and in our turn we grant the like;
　　　　but not so far that savages should mate with tame
　　　　or Serpents couple with birds, lambs with tigers.
　　　　　　　　　　Horace, *Epistle to the Pisos*, 11–15

This is what certain cabinets should say to the Europe that questions them.

as before the Revolution. Nevertheless, it would not have taken much for James II to regain his sceptre, and if he had had a bit more luck or only a little more tact, it would not have escaped him. Even though England had a king, even though religious prejudices united with political prejudices to exclude the Pretender, even though the geographical situation of the kingdom protected it from invasion, nevertheless, up until the middle of this century England faced the danger of a second revolution. It all depended, as we know, on the battle of Culloden.[7]

In France, on the other hand, the government is not monarchical; indeed, it is the enemy of all the neighbouring monarchies. It is not a prince who commands, and if the state is ever attacked, it does not appear likely that the foreign relatives of the pentarchs would raise troops to defend them. So France will be in constant danger of civil war. This danger has two obvious causes: the just rights of the Bourbons are always to be feared, and the astute policy of other powers will always be ready to try to profit from circumstances. As soon as the French throne is occupied by the legitimate sovereign no prince in the world could dream of seizing it, but as long as it is vacant it will be the object of covetousness and intrigue by every kind of royal ambition. Moreover, since it has been pushed to the dust, power is within the reach of anyone. Orderly government excludes an infinity of schemes, but under the rule of a false sovereignty there is no end of chimerical plots. All passions are unchained and every hope is licensed. The cowards who reject the king for fear of civil war are actually preparing the way for it. It is just because they foolishly desire stability and the constitution that they will have neither stability nor the constitution. There is no perfect security for France

7. [Charles Edward, the Stuart pretender, was defeated at the battle of Culloden in Scotland in 1746.]

in the present situation. Only the king, the legitimate king, wielding the sceptre of Charlemagne from the majesty of his throne, can dampen or disarm all these hatreds and outwit all these sinister plots. Only he by his command can make order of all these ambitions, calm excited minds, and suddenly surround authority with that magic wall which is its true guardian.

There is another consideration that must be kept before the eyes of those Frenchmen who are actually sharing authority and whose position enables them to influence the restoration of the monarchy. The more honourable of these men must not forget they will be carried along, sooner or later, by the force of things, that time flies, and that the chance for glory escapes them. That which they enjoy at the moment is a comparative glory: they put an end to the massacres; they tried to dry the nation's tears. They look good because they have succeeded the greatest scoundrels who ever soiled this globe. But when the throne has been restored for a hundred combined reasons, amnesty, in the full sense of the word, will be theirs. Their names, always obscure, will remain shrouded in oblivion. They should never lose sight of the immortal radiance that must surround the names of the monarchy's restorers. Every insurrection of the people against the nobility ends up in the creation of new nobles, and we have already seen how these new races, whose fame is created by circumstances and who from their creation will claim everything, are formed.

On the Property of the Nation

The question of the restitution of the property of the nation is being used to frighten the French; the king is blamed for not mentioning this delicate topic in his declaration.[8] One could say to a large majority of the nation, 'What does it matter to you?' and perhaps this would not be such a bad approach. But rather than give the impression of avoiding difficulties, I would point out that in this question of confiscated property the restoration of the monarchy agrees with the visible interests of France as a whole and even with the well-understood interests of the purchasers of the property in particular. The brigandage exercised with respect to these properties is evident to the most insensitive conscience. No one believes in the legitimacy of these acquisitions, and even those who have declaimed the most eloquently in favour of the present legislation have hastened to resell to ensure their profits. People do not dare enjoy these properties publicly, and the cooler people become to the idea, the less they will dare utilize these properties. The buildings will decay, and no one will dare build new ones for a long time; growth will be feeble, and French capital will dwindle considerably. Already this matter has caused a lot of trouble, and those who complain about the abuses of *decrees* must understand that this is a decree affecting perhaps a third of the most powerful kingdom in Europe.[9]

The deplorable condition of these properties has been described often enough in the legislative assembly. The problem will continue to worsen as long as the public conscience is troubled by doubts as to the soundness of these acquisitions. But who can see the end?

8. [*Biens nationaux:* this 'property of the nation' included confiscated church lands, crown lands, the king's personal domain, and confiscated estates of the émigrés. Much of this property had been sold to individuals who feared that restoration of the monarchy would mean its loss.]

9. [Maistre's estimate of a third is no doubt too high.]

Considering the possessors only, the leading danger for them comes from the government. Do not be deceived; which one is neither here nor there. The most unjust imaginable will ask no more than to fill its coffers in such a way as to make the least possible enemies. Moreover, everyone knows the conditions under which the buyers acquired these properties; everyone knows what infamous manoeuvring, what scandalous discounting, was involved. The initial and continuing defects of title are quite indelible. So the French government cannot help knowing that in putting pressure on these purchasers it will have public opinion on its side and that it will appear unjust only to the purchasers. Besides, under a popular government, even a legitimate one, injustice has no shame. One may judge what will happen in France, where the government, shifting with personalities and lacking identity, does not think of itself as going back on its word when it overthrows what has been done previously.

So it will turn to this confiscated property as soon as it is able to do so. Full of righteousness and (this must not be forgotten) of the jealousy of the have-nots for the haves, it will torment the possessors, either by new sales modified in some way or by general demands for price supplements or by extraordinary taxes. In other words, the possessors will never be left in peace.

But under a stable government everything is stable, so that even for the purchasers of this property it is important that the monarchy be restored in order that they know what they have. It is not at all fair to reproach the king for not having spoken clearly on this point in his declaration; he could not have done so without extreme imprudence. Perhaps when the time comes legislation will not be the best way to settle the problem.[10]

10. [In 1814–15, Louis XVIII had to ratify these acquisitions.]

But what I said in the preceding chapter must be recalled here: the conveniences of such-and-such class of individuals will not stop the counter-revolution. All I claim to prove is that it is to the advantage of the small number of men who can influence this great event not to wait until the accumulated abuses of anarchy make it inevitable, for the more necessary the king becomes, the harder will be the lot of all those who gained from the Revolution.

Of Vengeance

Another bugbear that has been used to make the French fear the return of their king is the vengeance with which his return must be accompanied. This objection, like the others, is usually made by intelligent men who do not believe it themselves; however, it is well to discuss it for the benefit of moderate Frenchmen who believe it well founded.

A number of royalist writers have rejected as an insult this supposed desire of vengeance on their part. Let one of them speak for all, and I cite him for my own pleasure as well as that of my readers. No one can accuse me of choosing a rigid royalist.

'Under the rule of an illegitimate power the most horrible vengeances are to be feared, for who would have the right to repress them? The victim can only call to his help the authority of laws that do not exist and a government that is only the creation of crime and usurpation.

'It is quite otherwise with a government placed firmly on sacred, ancient, and legitimate bases; it has the right to stifle the most just vengeance and to punish instantly with the sword of justice anyone who surrenders himself more to the sentiments of nature than to those of duty.

'Only a legitimate government has the right to proclaim an amnesty and the means to enforce it.

'It is demonstrable then that the most complete and purest royalist, the one whose relatives and properties have been the most grievously outraged, must be punished by death, if, under a legitimate government he dares revenge his own injuries when the king has demanded that he pardon them.

'Therefore it is under a government founded on our principles that amnesty can be securely accorded and severely observed.

'Ah, no doubt it would be easy to dispute the extent to which the king could extend his amnesty. The exceptions prescribed by his first duty are quite evident. All those guilty of Louis XVI's blood can only hope for God's pardon, but then who would dare trace exactly the limits of the king's amnesty and clemency? My heart and my pen both refuse to try. If anyone ever dares to write on this subject, it will no doubt be that rare and perhaps unique man, if he exists, who himself never erred in the course of this horrible revolution and whose heart, as pure as his conduct, has never needed pardon.'[11]

Reason and sentiment could not be expressed with more nobility. One would have to pity the man who could not recognize the accent of conviction in this piece.[12]

The month after the date of this work, the king in his declaration pronounced this sentence so renowned and so worthy of being known: 'Who would dare seek revenge when the king grants pardon?'

He excepted from amnesty only those who voted the

11. *Observations sur la conduite des puissances coalisées*, by the count d'Antraigues, avant-propos, pp. xxxiv ff.

12. [In fact, the count d'Antraigues was not an entirely dis-interested royalist. At the time Maistre wrote, d'Antraigues was operating a free-lance espionage network for profit, selling infor-mation to Spain, England, Austria, and other customers.]

death of Louis XVI, the cooperators, the direct and immediate instruments of his punishment, and the members of the revolutionary tribunal who sent the queen and Madame Elizabeth to the scaffold. Searching even to restrict the anathema in regard to the first, as much as conscience and honour would permit him, he did not count as parricides those of whom it might be thought 'that they associated with Louis XVI's assassins with the intention only of trying to save him'.

Even with regard 'to these monsters whom posterity will mention only with horror' the king contented himself with saying, with as much restraint as justice, 'All France calls the sword of justice down upon their heads.'

But by this phrase he did not deprive himself of his right to grant pardon in particular cases; it is up to the guilty to see what they can put in the balance to counterbalance their crime. Monk used Ingolsby to stop Lambert. It would be possible to do better than Ingolsby.[13]

Moreover, without detracting from the just horror due the murderers of Louis XVI, I would observe that in the eyes of divine justice all are not equally guilty. In morals as in physics, the force of fermentation is proportionate to the fermenting mass. Charles II's seventy judges were much more the masters of themselves than Louis XVI's judges. Certainly there were among the latter the consciously guilty who cannot be detested enough, but these great culprits had the skill to excite such a terror, they made such an impression on less vigorous minds, that many deputies were no doubt deprived of a part of their free will. It is difficult to form a clear idea of the indefinable and supernatural delirium that took possession of the assembly at the

13. [Ingolsby had been one of Charles I's judges. Nevertheless Monk used him against Lambert when the latter, a popular general under Cromwell, escaped from the Tower of London.]

time of Louis XVI's trial. I am convinced that many of the guilty, in remembering that dark time, think of it as a bad dream, that they are tempted to doubt what they did, and that they can no more explain it to themselves than we can explain it to them. These men, angry and surprised to be among the guilty, must try to make their peace.

In addition, this consideration applies to only a few; the nation would be quite mean if it regarded the punishment of such men as an obstacle to counter-revolution. But for those who worry about it, one may point out that Providence has already begun the punishment of the guilty; more than sixty regicides, the most guilty among them, have already died a violent death. No doubt others also will perish or flee Europe before France has a king; very few will fall into the hands of justice.

The French, quite calm about judicial revenge, must also be so about private vengeance; they have been given the most solemn promises in this regard. They have the king's word; they are not permitted to fear.

But since it is necessary to appeal to all men and to foresee all possible objections, since one must reply even to those who do not believe in honour and faith, it must be proved that private vengeance will not be possible.[14]

The most powerful sovereign has only two arms; his power depends on the instruments he uses and what he is given by public opinion. Moreover, even though it is evident that the king after the assumed restoration will want only to pardon, let us, to take things at their worst, make the entirely opposite supposition. How would he go

14. [There had, in fact, been a relatively large number of acts of private vengeance during the so-called White Terror in 1795. The second Restoration in 1815 (after Napoleon's Hundred Days) also saw a White Terror characterized by acts of personal vengeance.]

about it if he wanted to exercise arbitrary vengeance? Would the French army as we know it be a very pliant instrument in his hands? Ignorance and bad faith have been pleased to represent the future king as a Louis XIV, who like Homer's Jupiter, has only to lift an eyebrow to make France tremble. One hardly dare prove how false this supposition is. The power of sovereignty lies entirely in its moral force. It commands in vain if it does not possess this, and power must be possessed in its plenitude to be abused. The king of France who will ascend the throne of his ancestors surely will not wish to begin with abuses, and if he so wished it would be in vain because he would not be strong enough to fulfil the wish. The red bonnet, in touching the royal brow, has caused the sacred oil to disappear: the charm is broken, prolonged profanations have destroyed the divine rule of national prejudices, and for a long time to come, while cold reason may bind bodies, minds will remain standing. They claim to fear that the new king of France will deal severely with his enemies. The poor man, if he could only recompense his friends![15]

So the French have two infallible guarantees against the supposed vengeance which they fear—the king's interest and his impotence.[16]

15. Everyone knows Charles II's jest on the pleonasm of the English formula, amnesty and forgetfulness: 'I understand,' he said, 'amnesty for my enemies and oblivion for my friends.'

16. Events have justified all these sensible predictions. Since this work was completed, the French government has exposed two conspiracies and published documents by which the two, the one Jacobin, the other royalist, must be judged. In the Jacobin sheet it was written *Death to all our enemies*, and in the royalist *Pardon to all those who will not refuse it*. To keep people from drawing the consequences, they have said that the parlement must annul the royal amnesty. But this stupidity exceeds the *maximum*; surely it will not be believed. [Maistre's reference

The return of the émigrés furnishes the adversaries of the monarchy with another unfailing subject of imaginary fears, so it is important to dissipate this vision.

The first thing to remember is that there are true propositions whose truth depends on the period; however, they are repeated long after time has rendered them false and even ridiculous. The revolutionary party could have feared the return of the émigrés shortly after the passing of the laws that proscribed them. I do not concede that they were right, but what does it matter? It is a purely idle question now, useless to discuss. The question is to know if, *at the present moment*, the return of the émigrés is something dangerous for France.

The nobility sent two hundred eighty-four deputies to the Estates-General of fatal memory that produced all we have seen. According to a work on several bailiwicks there were never more than eighty electors for a deputy. It is not impossible that certain bailiwicks had a greater number present, but one must also take into account the individuals who voted in more than one bailiwick. All things considered, one can estimate at twenty-five thousand the number of heads of noble families who were represented in the Estates-General, and multiplying by five, the number we know is commonly attributed to each family, we have about one hundred twenty-five thousand noble heads. Let us say one hundred thirty thousand, to take the highest possible number. Take away the women, leaving sixty-five thousand. Subtract from this number (1) the nobles who never left, (2) those who have already returned, (3) the

---

to a 'Jacobin' conspiracy probably refers to Babeuf's Conspiracy of the Equals. The second involved an attempt by a royalist organization to foment insurrection among troops stationed in Paris. The Directory learned of the plot, set a trap, and arrested four royalist agents who were tried in March of 1797.]

dotards, (4) the children, (5) the sick, (6) the priests, and (7) all those who have perished as a result of war, punishment, or purely natural causes. What will be left is a number that is hard to determine exactly, but that from any point of view whatever could not alarm France.

A prince worthy of his name led five thousand, or at most six thousand, men into combat. This corps, which was not even composed entirely of nobles, gave proof of admirable valour under foreign colours, but if it was isolated it would disappear.[17] So it is clear that, militarily, the émigrés are nothing and can do nothing.

There is one additional consideration that is more particularly related to the spirit of this work and that merits development.

Nothing happens by chance in this world, and even in a secondary sense there is no disorder, for disorder is commanded by a sovereign hand that submits it to a rule and forces it to contribute to a good.

A revolution is only a political movement that has to produce a certain effect in a certain time. Movement has its laws, and observing it carefully over a certain period of time one can draw certain enough conclusions for the future. Now one of the laws of the French Revolution is that the émigrés can attack it only at their own misfortune and that they are totally excluded from whatever work they undertake.

From the first dream of counter-revolution to the ever-lamentable Quiberon expedition, nothing they have tried has succeeded and their efforts have even turned against them. Not only do they not succeed, but everything they

17. [The prince de Condé had a considerable army in the Rhineland in 1792, but by 1796 this group had withered away to a relatively small band. Maistre, in effect, is recommending that they disband.]

try is marked by such powerlessness and nullity that public opinion has become accustomed to regarding them as men who obstinately defend a proscribed party. This has thrown them into a disfavour that even their friends perceive. And this disfavour will not surprise men who think that the principal cause of the French Revolution was the moral degradation of the nobility.

M. de Saint-Pierre observed somewhere in his *Etudes de la nature* that if one compares the appearance of French nobles to that of their ancestors whose features have been handed down to us by painting or sculpture, one can see evidence that these families have degenerated. He is more to be believed on this point than on polar fusions and the shape of the earth.[18]

In every state, even in monarchies, there is a certain number of families who can be called *co-sovereigns*, for the nobility is only an extension of sovereignty in such governments. These families are the depositories of a sacred fire that will be extinguished if they lose their purity.

It is questionable if these families, once extinguished, can be perfectly replaced. At least it is not necessary to believe that sovereigns can *ennoble*, if we use the term precisely. There are new families that spring up in the administration of the state, that extricate themselves from the common herd in a striking manner, and that arise from among others like a tall sturdy tree in the middle of the brush.[19] Sovereigns may sanction these natural ennoble-

18. [Bernardin de Saint-Pierre, *Etudes de la Nature* (Paris: 1784). Saint-Pierre attributed the biblical flood to an 'effusion' of polar ice.]

19. [Perhaps an allusion to Joseph de Maistre's own family. His paternal grandfather had been a cloth merchant in Nice; his father had received the title of count for his work in codifying the laws of Savoy.]

ments, but if they allow themselves to approve too many on their own authority, they work for the destruction of their states. Fraudulent nobility was one of the greatest evils of France; other less brilliant empires are weakened and dis-honoured by it while awaiting other misfortunes.

Modern philosophy, which likes to talk of *chance* so much, speaks especially of the chance of *birth*; this is one of its favourite texts. But there is no more chance here than in other matters. There are noble families just as there are sovereign families. Can a man make a sovereign? At most he may be used as an instrument for the deposition of one sovereign and the transfer of his state to another sovereign who is already a prince.[20] Furthermore, there has never existed a sovereign family to which one can assign a plebe-ian origin; if this phenomena should appear it would be epoch-making.[21]

Scale considered, it is the same with nobility as with sovereignty. Without going into all the details, let us just note that if the nobility renounces the national dogmas, the state is lost.[22]

20. And even the way in which human power is used in this circumstance is such as to humiliate it. On this point especially, one may address man with Rousseau's words, *Show me your power, and I will show you your weakness.*

21. We often hear it said, 'If Richard Cromwell had had his father's genius, he would have made the Protectorate hereditary in his family.' How true!

22. An Italian scholar has made a singular remark. After observing that the nobility is the natural guardian and, in a sense, the depository of the national religion, and that this phenomenon is more striking the farther back one goes towards the origins of nations and things, he adds, 'So it has to be a great sign that the nation's end has come when the nobles despise the native religion.' Vico, *Principi d'una Scienza nuova*, Bk. II. When the priesthood is part of the state's political structure, and

The role played by some nobles in the French Revolution is a thousand times more *terrible* (I do not say more horrible) than anything else we have seen in the Revolution. There is no more frightening, no more decisive sign of the dreadful judgement brought against the French monarchy.

Perhaps it will be asked what these faults have in common with the émigrés who detest them? I reply that the individuals who compose nations, families, and even political bodies form a unity; this is a fact. In the second place I reply that the causes of the suffering of the émigré nobility are quite anterior to the Revolution. The difference that we see between such-and-such French nobles is, in God's eyes, only a difference of longitude and latitude; it is not because one is here or there that one is what one must be. *Not all those who cry Lord! Lord! will enter into the kingdom.* Men can judge only by appearances; but a given noble at Koblenz may have more reason for self-reproach than a given noble who sat on the left in the so-called constituent assembly. Finally, the French nobility has only itself to blame for all its troubles, and when it accepts this fact it will have taken one great step forward. The exceptions, more or less numerous, are worthy of the world's respect, but one can speak only in general terms. Today the unfortunate nobility (who can suffer only an eclipse) must bow its head and resign itself. Some day it will have to embrace in good faith the children who are not its own. While waiting, it must make no more exterior efforts; perhaps it would even be desirable that they never be seen in a menacing attitude. In any case, emigration was an error,

---

its highest offices are normally occupied by the high nobility, the result is the strongest and most durable of all possible constitutions. So it was that philosophism, the universal solvent, passed its crucial test with the French monarchy.

not a crime; the majority thought they were obeying honour. *Numen abire jubet; prohibent discedere leges.*[23] God must absolve them.

There are many other comments one could make on this point, but let us restrict ourselves to what is obvious. The émigrés can do nothing, and one can even add that they are nothing, for every day, despite the government, their number diminishes according to the invariable law of the French Revolution that wills that everything happens despite men and against all probabilities.

Long misfortunes having softened the émigrés, every day they become more like their fellow citizens, bitterness disappears, and on one side and then another they begin to recall their common fatherland. A hand is extended, and even on the field of battle the other is recognized as brother. The strange amalgam that we have seen for some time has no visible cause, for these laws are not visible, but it is no less real. Therefore it is obvious that the number of the émigrés count for nothing. As for the more violent passions of a small number of men, we may neglect worrying about them.[24]

But there is one more important point that I must not pass over in silence. References are made to some imprudent speeches made by young men, thoughtless or embittered by misfortune, in order to frighten the French on the return of these men. I agree, to put all the suppositions against me, these discourses really announce well-decided intentions. But can we believe that those who hold them will be in a situation to execute them after the restoration of the monarchy? That would be to be badly deceived. From the very moment the legitimate government is

23. Ovid, *Metamorphoses*, XV, 28. [The god bade him depart; his country's laws prohibited his departure.]

24. [An explicit disavowal of the ultraroyalists.]

restored these men will be powerless to do anything but obey. Anarchy is necessary for revenge; order severely excludes it. The man who at the moment talks only of punishment will then find himself in circumstances that will force him to want only what the law wants, and for his own interest, even he will be a quiet citizen and leave vengeance to the courts. People are always dazzled by the same sophism: 'One party dealt harshly when it ruled; therefore the opposite party will deal harshly when it gets its turn to rule.' Nothing is more false. In the first place, the sophism supposes that both parties have the same vices. This is assuredly not the case. Without insisting too much on the virtues of the royalists, I am sure that I have the world's conscience with me when I simply affirm that there are fewer virtues on the republican side. Besides, even their prejudices, apart from their virtues, ensure that France can suffer from the royalists nothing similar to what it underwent from their enemies.

Already experience provides a prelude to calm the French on this point; they have seen on more than one occasion that the party that suffered everything at the hands of its enemies has not known how to revenge itself when it held its enemies in its power. A few acts of vengeance that caused a great furore prove the same proposition, for it can be seen that only the most scandalous denial of justice can lead to this vengeance and that no one will try to take justice into his own hands if the government can carry it out as well.

There is, moreover, great evidence that the most pressing interest of the king will be to prevent such revenge. Just emerging from the evils of anarchy it is unlikely that he would want to return to it. The very idea of violence will make him pale, and this is the one crime that he will not believe himself capable of pardoning.

In addition France is ready to forsake convulsions and horrors; it wants no more blood. And since public opinion is strong enough at the moment to compromise the party that would want it, one can judge the force of this public opinion when it has the government on its side. After prolonged and terrible evils Frenchmen will be delighted to place themselves in the arms of the monarchy. Any attack on this tranquillity will truly be a crime of *lèse-nation* that the courts would perhaps not have time to punish.

These reasons are so convincing that no one can be mistaken. Moreover, one must not be duped by these writings in which we see a hypocritical philanthropy condemn the horrors of the Revolution and then argue from these excesses to establish the necessity of preventing a second. In fact they condemn the Revolution only in order not to excite a universal outcry against themselves; but they love it, they love its authors and its results, and of all the crimes that it spawned they scarcely condemn those with which they could dispense. There is not one of these writings in which one does not find obvious proofs that the authors are inclined to the party they are condemning through shame.

Thus the French, always dupes, are duped on this occasion more than ever; they experience a general fear when they have nothing to fear, and they sacrifice their happiness to satisfy a few miserable rascals.

But if the most obvious theories cannot convince the French, and if they still cannot bring themselves to believe that Providence is the guardian of order and that it is not at all the same thing if one works for it or against it, let us at least judge what will happen by what has happened. And if reasoning eludes our minds let us at least believe history, which is experimental politics. England in the last century presents almost the same spectacle as France in ours. There the fanaticism of liberty, overexcited by that of religion, penetrated souls even more deeply than it has in France, where the cult of liberty has no basis at all. Moreover, what a difference in the character of the two nations and in that of the actors who have played a role on these two stages! Where are, I do not say the Hampdens,[25] but the Cromwells, of France? And nevertheless, despite the burning fanaticism of the republicans, despite the deliberate steadfastness of the national character, despite the too-understandable errors of numerous guilty persons and especially of the army, did the restoration of the monarchy in England cause splits similar to those which had spawned a regicide revolution? Show us the atrocious vengeance of the royalists. A few regicides perished under the authority of the law; for the rest, there were neither combats nor private revenge. The return of the king was marked only by a cry of joy which included all England; enemies all embraced one another. The king, surprised by what he saw, was moved to exclaim, 'It is not my fault if I have been rejected so long by such a good people.' The illustrious Clarendon, a witness and reliable historian of these great events, tells us 'that a man could not help but wonder where those people dwelt who had done all the mischief and kept the king from enjoying the comfort and support of such excellent subjects for so many years'.[26] Which is to say the *people* no longer recognized the *people*. It could not be better said.

But what brought about this great change? Nothing, or rather, nothing visible. A year before none believed it possible. It is not even known if it was begun by a royalist;

25. Hume, Vol. XX, ch. lxxii, the year 1660.

26. [Clarendon, 1st earl of, Edward Hyde (1609–74). His *History of the Rebellion and Civil Wars in England* was written in France after his exile in 1667 and published 1702–04.]

for it is an insoluble problem to know when Monk began to serve the monarchy in good faith. But was it not at least a matter of the royalist party imposing a change on the opposite party? Not at all. Monk had only six thousand men; the republicans had five or six times as many, and they occupied all the offices and were in military occupation of the entire kingdom. Nevertheless Monk did not have to fight a single battle; everything was accomplished effortlessly and as if by magic. It will be the same in France. The return to order will not be painful, because it will be natural and because it will be favoured by a secret force whose action is wholly creative. We will see precisely the opposite of what we have seen. Instead of these violent commotions, painful divisions, and perpetual and desperate oscillations, a certain stability, and indefinable peace, a universal well-being will announce the presence of sovereignty. There will be no shocks, no violence, no punishment even, except those which the true nation will approve. Even crime and usurpation will be treated with a measured severity, with a calm justice that belongs to legitimate power only. The king will bind up the wounds of the state with a gentle and paternal hand. In conclusion, this is the great truth with which the French cannot be too greatly impressed: the restoration of the monarchy, what they call the counter-revolution, will be not a *contrary revolution*, but the *contrary of revolution*.

XI

From a History of the English Revolution by David Hume

Eadem Mutata Resurgo

[I rise again, transformed, but the same]

The Long Parliament declared by a solemn oath that it could not be dissolved (p. 181). To assure its power, it never ceased stirring up the people, sometimes inflaming their minds by cunning speeches (p. 176), sometimes causing petitions in support of the Revolution to be sent in from all

I cite the Basel English edition, 12 volumes, Legrand, 1789. [Maistre's method in this chapter is to put together passages from Hume's *History of England* so as to show parallels between events in England and the French Revolution. Maistre's translation from Hume's English was generally accurate, though he sometimes shortened passages considerably. In rendering this chapter into English again, I have often used Hume's words when I could find them, but in other cases I have simply translated Maistre's French into English. My aim has been to preserve the effect that Maistre's chapter would have had for French readers. On the use made of Hume by counter-revolutionary writers, see L. L. Bongie, *David Hume, Prophet of Counter-Revolution* (Oxford: Clarendon Press, 1965).]

parts of the realm (p. 133). Abuse in the press was carried to extremes; numerous clubs everywhere produced noisy tumults; fanaticism had its own language, it was a new jargon invented by the fury and hypocrisy of the times (p. 131). Every day produced some new harangue on past grievances (p. 129). All the old institutions were overthrown one after the other (pp. 125, 188). The *self-denial* ordinance and the *new model* bill completely disorganized the army and gave it a new form and new composition which forced many old officers to resign their commissions (p. 13). Every kind of crime was attributed to the royalists (p. 148), and the art of deceiving and frightening the people was carried to the point of making them believe that the royalists had mined the Thames (p. 177). No king, no nobility, universal equality, became the watchwords (p. 87). But in the midst of this popular effervescence, there now appeared a separate party, the *Independents*, an enthusiastic sect which ended by enslaving the Long Parliament (p. 186).

Against such a storm, the goodness of the king proved useless; the very concessions which he granted his people were calumniated as having been made in bad faith (p. 186).

It is by these preliminaries that the rebels prepared the fall of Charles I; but a simple assassination would not have fulfilled their design: the crime would not have been national; the shame and danger would have fallen on the murderers only. So it was necessary to conceive another plan, it was necessary to astonish the world with an unheard-of procedure, to make an exterior show of justice and cover cruelty with audacity; it was, in short, necessary to fanaticize the people with notions of perfect equality, to assure the obedience of the masses, and gradually to form a coalition against the monarchy (vol. 10, p. 91).

The destruction of the monarchy was the preliminary to the death of the king. The king was in reality dethroned and the English constitution overthrown (in 1648) by the vote of non-addresses which separated the king from the constitution.

Soon the blackest and most ridiculous calumnies about the king were spread about to kill that respect which is the safeguard of thrones. The rebels omitted nothing that might sully his reputation; they accused him of having delivered fortresses to England's enemies, of having spilled his subjects' blood. It was by calumny that they prepared themselves for violence (p. 94).

During the king's imprisonment at Carisbrooke Castle, the usurpers took it upon themselves to subject their unfortunate prince to every kind of hardship. They removed all his servants, they cut off his correspondence with his friends; no amusement was allowed him, nor society, which might relieve his anxious thoughts. At every moment he expected to be assassinated or poisoned,[1] for the idea of a judicial sentence never entered his thoughts (pp. 59, 95).

While the king suffered cruelly from his imprisonment, Parliament was very industrious in publishing how cheerful the king was, how satisfied he was with his present condition.[2]

The great source whence the king derived consolation amidst all his calamities was undoubtedly religion. The king's religion seems to have contained nothing fierce or gloomy, nothing which enraged him against his adversaries, or terrified him with the dismal prospect of futurity. While everything around him bore a hostile aspect; while friends, family, relations were separated from him and unable to serve him, he reposed himself with confidence in

1. This was also Louis XVI's expectation. See his historical eulogy.

2. We recall having read in Condorcet's newspaper a piece about the king's good appetite on his return from Varennes.

the arms of that Being who penetrates and sustains all nature, and whose severities, received with piety and resignation, appeared to the king as the surest pledges of unexhausted favour (pp. 95, 96).

The men of law conducted themselves badly in this circumstance. Bradshaw, a member of this profession, was not ashamed to preside at the court which condemned the king, and Coke became solicitor for the people of England (p. 123). The court was composed of officers of the rebellious army, members of the lower house, and citizens of London, most of them of mean birth (p. 123).

Charles doubted not that he would die; he knew that a king is rarely dethroned without perishing, but he expected murder rather than a solemn trial (p. 122).

In his prison he was already dethroned: all the exterior symbols of sovereignty were withdrawn, and his attendants had orders to serve him without ceremony (p. 122). He soon reconciled himself to rudeness and familiarities as he had done to his other calamities (p. 123).

The king's judges styled themselves *representatives of the people* (p. 124), . . . of the people, the only source of every lawful power (p. 127), and the act of accusation represented that having abused the limited power with which he had been entrusted, he [Charles Stuart] *had traitorously and maliciously erected an unlimited and tyrannical government on the ruins of liberty*.

After the charge was finished, the president told the king that he could speak (p. 125). Charles answered with great temper and dignity (p. 125). It is confessed that the king's behaviour during this last scene of his life does honour to his memory (p. 127). Firm and intrepid, he maintained in all his answers the utmost perspicuity and justness both of thought and expression (p. 128). Mild and equable, he rose into no passion at that unusual authority which was assumed over him. His soul, without effort or affectation, seemed only to remain in the situation familiar to it, and to look with contempt on all the efforts of human malice and iniquity (p. 128).

The people, in general, remained in that silence which great passions produce in the human mind. The soldiers, being incessantly plied with all sorts of seductions, were wrought up to a degree of fury, and imagined that the frightful crime with which they soiled themselves was a title of glory (p. 130).

Three days were allowed the king; this interval he passed with great tranquillity, chiefly in reading and devotion. His family were allowed access to him and they received many pious consolations and advises (p. 130). Every night during this interval the king slept as sound as usual. The morning of the fatal day he rose early and employed more than usual care in dressing. A minister of religion, a man endowed with the same mild and steady virtues by which the king himself was so much distinguished, assisted him in his last moments (p. 132).

The street before Whitehall was the place destined for the execution; for it was intended, by choosing that very place in sight of his own palace, to display more evidently the triumph of popular justice over royal majesty. When the king came upon the scaffold, he found it so surrounded by soldiers, that he could not expect to be heard by any of the people: he addressed therefore, his discourse to the few persons who were about him. He forgave all his enemies and accused none; he expressed his wishes for his people. A prelate who was assisting him called to him, 'There is, sire, but one stage more, which though troublesome, is yet a very short one; it will carry you from earth to heaven.' 'I go', replied the king, 'from a corruptible to an incorruptible crown, where no disturbance can have place.'

From a History by David Hume   175

At one blow was his head severed from his body. The executioner held up to the spectators the head, streaming with blood, and cried aloud, 'This is the head of a traitor!' (pp. 132, 133).

This prince deserves the epithet of a *good*, rather than of a *great* man. At times his good sense was disfigured by a deference to persons of a capacity inferior to his own. He was more fitted to rule in a regular established government, than either to give way or to subdue the encroachments of a popular assembly (p. 136). If he lacked the courage to act he always had courage to suffer. Unhappily, his fate threw him into a difficult period; and if his political prudence was not sufficient to extricate himself from so perilous a situation, he may be excused; since, even after the event, when it is commonly easy to correct all errors, one is at a loss to know what he should have done (p. 137). Exposed without assistance to the assault of the most furious and implacable factions, it was never permitted him, but with the most fatal consequences, to commit the smallest mistake; a condition too rigorous to be imposed on the greatest human capacity (p. 137).

Some historians have rashly questioned the good faith of this prince; but, for this reproach, the most malignant scrutiny of his conduct, which in every circumstance is now thoroughly known, affords not any reasonable foundation. On the contrary, if we consider the extreme difficulties to which he was so frequently reduced, and compare his conduct to his declarations, we shall avow, that probity and honour ought justly to be numbered among his most shining qualities (p. 137).

The death of the king put a seal on the destruction of the monarchy. It was abolished by a decree of the commons. The commons ordered a new great seal to be engraved with this legend: *On the first year of freedom.* The forms of all public business were changed, from the king's name, to that of the keepers of the liberties of England (p. 142). The *court of king's bench* was called the *court of public bench*. The king's statue in the Exchange was thrown down, and on the pedestal these words were inscribed: *Exit tyrannus, regum ultimus* (p. 143).

Charles, in dying, left his people an image of himself (*Eikon Basilike*)[3] in that famous work, a masterpiece of elegance, purity, neatness, and simplicity. It is not easy to conceive the general compassion excited towards the king, by the publishing of a work so full of piety, meekness, and humanity. Many have not scrupled to ascribe to that book the subsequent restoration of the royal family (p. 146).

It is seldom that the people gain anything by revolutions in government; because the new settlement, jealous and insecure, must commonly be supported with more expense and severity than the old (p. 100).

On no occasion was the truth of this maxim more sensibly felt, than in the present situation in England. Complaints against the oppression of ship money, against the tyranny of the star chamber, had roused the people to arms: and having gained a complete victory over the crown, they found themselves loaded with a multiplicity of taxes, formerly unknown; and scarcely an appearance of law and liberty remained in the administration. Every office was entrusted to the most ignoble part of the nation; a base populace exalted above their superiors; hypocrites, exercising iniquity under the visor of religion (p. 100). The loan of great sums of money was exacted from all such as lay under any suspicion. Never had England known a more severe and

3. [*Eikon Basilike* (Greek for 'royal image'), a book purporting to be the spiritual autobiography of the king, was published shortly after the king's execution.]

arbitrary government, than was exercised by the patrons of liberty (pp. 112, 113).

The first act of the Long Parliament had been an oath by which it had declared that it could never be dissolved (p. 181).

The confusions which overspread England after the execution of Charles I, proceeded less from the spirit of innovation which agitated the ruling party than from the dissolution of all old authority. Every man had framed the model of a republic; and however new it was, or fantastical, he was eager in recommending it to his fellow-citizens, or even imposing it by force. Each plan, being founded on supposed inspiration, not any principles of human reason, had no means, besides cant and low rhetoric, by which it could recommend itself to others (p. 147). The *levellers* disclaimed all dependence and subordination.[4] One particular sect expected the millennium;[5] the *Antinomians* insisted that the obligations of morality and natural law were suspended. A considerable party declaimed against the tithes and a hireling priesthood, and were resolved that the magistrate should not support by power or revenue any ecclesiastical establishment; each should have the liberty of supporting the one he preferred. All religions should be tolerated, except Catholicism. Another party inveighed against the law and its professors; and, on pretence of rendering more simple the distribution of justice, were desirous of abolishing the whole system of English jurisprudence, which seemed interwoven with monarchical government (p. 148). Ardent republicans changed their

4. 'We want a government . . . where distinctions are born only of equality, where the citizen is submissive to the magistrate, the magistrate to the people, and the people to justice.' Robespierre. See the *Moniteur*, 7 February 1794.

5. This particular parallel should not be lightly overlooked.

baptismal names, substituting for them names as extravagant as their spirit of revolution (p. 242). They decided that marriage was a simple contract, which must be celebrated before the civil magistrates. There is even a legend in England that they carried their fanaticism to the point of suppressing the word *kingdom* in the Lord's Prayer, saying *thy republic come*. Cromwell entertained a project of instituting a college, in imitation of that of Rome, for the *propagation* of the faith (p. 285).

Even the less fanatical republicans supposed themselves above all laws, professions, and oaths. The bands of society were everywhere loosened; and the irregular passions of men were encouraged by speculative principles, still more unsocial and irregular (p. 148).

The royalists, being degraded from their authority and plundered of their property, were inflamed with the highest resentment and indignation against those ignoble adversaries who had reduced them to subjection. From inclination and principle, they zealously attached themselves to the son of their unfortunate monarch, whose memory they respected and whose tragic death they deplored.

On the other hand, the Presbyterians, the founders of the republic, whose credit had first supported the arms of the parliament, were enraged to find that, by the treachery or superior cunning of their associates, the fruits of all their successful labours were ravished from them. This discontent pushed them towards the royalists without winning them over completely; they still had many prejudices to overcome, many fears and jealousies to be allayed, ere they could cordially entertain thoughts of restoring the family which they had so grievously offended.

After having murdered their sovereign with so many appearing circumstances of solemnity and justice, and so much real violence and even fury, these men began to think of giving themselves a more regular form of government. They named a council of state which was accorded executive authority. This council gave orders to all the generals and admirals, received all addresses, executed the laws, and digested all business before it was introduced into Parliament (pp. 150–51). The administration was divided among several committees which tried to engross everything (p. 134) and rendered account to none (pp. 166–67).

The usurpers of authority, both by the turn of their disposition and by the nature of the instruments which they employed, were better qualified for acts of force and vigour than for the slow and deliberate work of legislation; nevertheless, the men of the assembly pretended to employ themselves with legislation for the country. They worked on a new plan of representation; and as soon as they should have settled the nation, they professed their intention of restoring the power to the people, from whom they acknowledged they had entirely derived it (p. 151).

In the meantime, the parliament judged it necessary to enlarge the laws against treason beyond those narrow bounds within which they had been confined during the monarchy. They even comprehended verbal offences, nay, intentions, though they never appeared in any overt act against the state. To affirm the present government to be a usurpation, to assert that the parliament or council of state was tyrannical or illegal, to endeavour subverting their authority, or stirring up sedition against them: these offences were declared to be high treason. The power of imprisonment, which had been taken from the king, it was found necessary to restore to the council of state; and all the jails in England were filled with men whom the jealousies and fears of the ruling party had represented as dangerous (p. 163).

It was great sport for these new masters to deprive the landed nobility of their titles; when the brave Montrose was executed in Scotland, James Graham was the only name his judges vouchsafed to give him (p. 180).

Besides the customs and excise, ninety thousand pounds a month were levied on land for the subsistence of the army. The sequestrations and compositions of the royalists, the sale of the crown lands, and of the dean and chapter lands, though they yielded great sums, were not sufficient to support the vast expenses, and as was suspected, the great depredations, of the parliament and of their creatures (pp. 163–64).

Even the royal palaces were pulled in pieces, and the materials in them sold. All the king's furniture was put to sale: his pictures, disposed of at very low prices, enriched all the collections of Europe; pieces which had cost 50,000 guineas were given away for 300 (p. 388).

The republicans acquired little popularity or credit. These men had not that large thought nor those comprehensive views, which might qualify them for acting the part of legislators. Egotists and hypocrites, they made small progress in fixing a plan of government, so that the nation began to apprehend that they intended to establish themselves as a perpetual legislature, and to confine the whole power to sixty or seventy persons, who called themselves the *parliament of the commonwealth of England*. While they pretended to bestow new liberties upon the nation, they found themselves obliged to infringe even the most valuable of those, which, through time immemorial, had been transmitted from their ancestors. Not daring to entrust the trials of treason to juries, who would have been little favourable to the commonwealth, the parliament erected a high court of justice, which was to receive indictments from the council of state (pp. 206–7). This court was composed of men devoted to the ruling party, without name or character, determined to sacrifice everything to their own safety or ambition.

As for royalists taken prisoners in battle, they were put to death by sentence of court martial (p. 207).

The only solid support of the republican independent faction which, though it formed so small a part of the nation, had violently usurped the government of the whole, was a numerous army (p. 149). Such is the influence of established government, that the commonwealth, though founded in usurpation the most unjust and unpopular, had authority sufficient to raise everywhere the militia of the counties; and these, united with the regular forces, bent all their efforts against the king (p. 199). At Newbury (in 1643) the militia of London equalled what could be expected from the most veteran forces. The officers preached to the soldiers and they marched to battle singing fanatical hymns (p. 13).

A numerous army served equally to retain everyone in implicit subjection to established authority, and to strike a terror into foreign nations. The power of peace and war was lodged in the same hands with that of imposing taxes. The military genius of the people had, by the civil contests, been roused from its former lethargy. The confusion into which all things had been thrown, had given opportunity to men of low stations to break through obscurity, and to raise themselves by their courage to commands which they were well qualified to exercise, but to which their birth could never have entitled them (p. 209). We see a man of fifty (Blake) suddenly transfer from the land service to the navy and distinguish himself in the most brilliant manner (p. 210). During the variety of ridiculous and distracted scenes which the civil government exhibited in England, the military force was exerted with vigour, conduct, and unanimity; and never did the kingdom appear more formidable to all foreign nations (p. 248).

A government totally military and despotic, is almost sure, after some time, to fall into impotence and languor; but when it immediately succeeds a legal constitution, it may, at first, to foreign nations appear very vigorous and active, and may exert with more unanimity that power, spirit, and riches, which had been acquired under a better form. This was the spectacle which England presented at that time. The moderate temper and unwarlike genius of the last two princes, the extreme difficulties under which they laboured at home, and the great security which they enjoyed from foreign enemies, had rendered them negligent of the transactions on the continent; and England had been, in a manner, overlooked in the general system of Europe; but the republican government suddenly put it in the forefront again (p. 263). Notwithstanding the late war and bloodshed, the power of England had never, in any period, appeared so formidable to the neighbouring kingdoms (p. 209), and to foreign nations (p. 218). The weight of England, even under its most legal and bravest princes, was never more sensibly felt than during this unjust and violent usurpation (p. 263).

The parliament, elated by successes, thought that everything must yield to their fortunate arms; they treated second-rate powers with great haughtiness, and for real or claimed offences, declared war or demanded solemn satisfaction (p. 221).

This famous parliament, which had filled all Europe with the renown of its actions, and with astonishment at its crimes, nevertheless allowed itself to be enslaved by a single man (p. 128); and foreign nations stood astonished to see a nation, so turbulent and unruly, who, for some doubtful encroachments on their privileges, had dethroned and murdered an excellent prince, descended from a long line of monarchs, now at last subdued and reduced to slavery by one who, a few years before was no better than a private gentleman, whose name was not known in the nation, and who was little regarded even in that low sphere to which he had always been confined (p. 236).[6]

The conduct of this same tyrant in foreign affairs drew a consideration to his country, which, since the reign of Elizabeth, it seemed to have totally lost. He seemed to ennoble, instead of debasing, that people whom he had reduced to subjection, and their national vanity, being gratified, made them bear with more patience all the indignities and calamities under which they laboured (pp. 280–81).

It seems now proper to look abroad to the general state of Europe, and to consider the measures which England at this time embraced in its negotiations with the neighbouring princes (p. 262).

Richelieu was first minister in France. His emissaries had furnished fuel to the flame of rebellion when it first broke out; but after the conflagration had diffused itself, the French court, observing the materials to be of themselves sufficiently combustible, found it unnecessary any longer to animate the British malcontents to an opposition to their sovereign. On the contrary, they offered their mediation for composing the internal disorders; and their ambassadors, from decency, pretended to act in concert with the court of England in exile (p. 264).

6. 'So little were these men endowed with the spirit of legislation that they boasted that they had employed only four days in drawing this instrument which placed Cromwell at the head of the republic.' (Ibid.) The Constitution of 1795 may be recalled here. As they said in Paris after the fall of its makers, *it was made in a few days by a few juveniles.*

Nevertheless, Charles received but few civilities, and still less support, from the French court (pp. 170, 266). One morning the Princess Henrietta was obliged to lie abed for want of a fire to warm her. To such a condition was reduced, in the midst of Paris, a queen of England, and daughter of Henry IV of France (p. 266).

They treated Charles with such affected indifference, that he thought it more decent to withdraw, and prevent the indignity of being desired to leave the kingdom (p. 267).

Spain was the first Power that recognized the republic, even though its royal family was related to that of England. It sent an ambassador to London and received one from the parliament (p. 208).

Sweden having at this time achieved the height of its greatness, the new republic anxiously courted the alliance of this power and obtained it (p. 263).

The king of Portugal had dared close his ports to the republican admiral; but soon dreading so dangerous a foe to his newly-acquired dominion, and sensible of the unequal contest in which he was engaged, made all possible submissions to the haughty republic, and was at last admitted to negotiate the renewal of his alliance with England.

The people in the United Provinces were much attached to Charles's interests. Besides his connection with the family of Orange, which was extremely beloved by the populace, all men regarded with compassion his helpless condition, and expressed the greatest abhorrence against the murder of his father. But the states were uneasy at his presence. They dreaded the parliament, so formidable in its power, and so prosperous in all its enterprises. They apprehended the most precipitate resolutions from such violent and haughty dispositions, and they found it necessary to satisfy the English commonwealth, by removing the king to a distance from them (p. 169).

Cardinal Mazarin was artful and vigilant, supple and patient, false and intriguing. All circumstances of respect were paid to the daring usurper, who had imbrued his hands in the blood of his sovereign, a prince so nearly related to the royal family of France. Mazarin wrote to Cromwell and *expressed his regret that his urgent affairs should deprive him of the honour which he had long wished for, of paying in person his respects to the greatest man in world* (p. 307).

Cromwell treated as an equal with the French king, and in a treaty between the two nations, the protector's name was inserted before that of Louis XIV in that copy which remained in England (p. 268, note).

The Prince Palatine much neglected his uncle, and paid court to the parliament; he accepted a pension of eight thousand pounds a year from them, and took a place in their assembly of divines (p. 263, note). Such was the ascendancy of the republic with foreign princes.

And in England itself, there were great numbers at that time who made it a principle always to adhere to any power which was uppermost, and to support the established government (p. 239). At the head of this system was the illustrious and gallant Blake, who said to his seamen, *It is still our duty to fight for our country, into what hands soever the government may fall* (p. 279).

Against an order of things so well established, the royalists were reduced to dubious ventures which turned against them. The government had spies everywhere, and it was not difficult to obtain intelligence of a confederacy so generally diffused, among a party who valued themselves more on zeal and courage, than on secrecy and sobriety (p. 259). The royalists fancied that everyone who was dissatisfied like them, had also embraced the same views and inclinations. They did not consider that the old parliamentary party, though many of them were displeased with Cromwell, who had dispossessed them of their power, were still more apprehensive of any success to the royal cause; whence besides a certain prospect of the same consequence, they had so much reason to dread the severest vengeance for their past transgressions (p. 259).

The situation of the royalist conspirators was deplorable. Their very conspiracies were regarded as a fortunate event since they justified tyrannical severities. Many of the royalists were thrown into prison; an edict was issued exacting the tenth penny from the whole party, in order to make them pay the expenses to which their mutinous disposition continually exposed the public. All the royalists were obliged anew to redeem themselves by great sums of money; and many of them were reduced by these multiplied disasters to extreme poverty. Whoever was known to be disaffected, or even lay under any suspicion, was exposed to the new exaction (pp. 260–61).

Near one half of the goods and chattels, and at least one half of the lands, rents, and revenues of the kingdom, had been sequestered. Besides pitying the ruin and desolation of so many ancient and honourable families, indifferent spectators could not but blame the hardship of punishing with such severity actions which the law strictly required of every subject (pp. 66–67). The severities exercised against the Episcopal clergy were no less; by the most moderate computation, it appears that above one half of the established clergy had been turned out to beggary and want, for no other crime than their adhering to the civil and religious principles in which they had been educated, and for their attachment to those laws under whose countenance they had at first embraced that profession (p. 67).

The royalists had been instructed by the king to remain quiet, and to cover themselves under the appearance of republicans (p. 254). For himself, poor and neglected, he wandered Europe, changing his place of exile according to circumstance and consoling himself for present calamities with the hope of a better future (p. 152).

The condition of that monarch, to all the world, seemed totally desperate, the more so that, seeming to seal his fate, all the commons had signed without hesitation an engagement not to alter the present government (p. 325).[7] His friends had been baffled in every attempt for his service: the scaffold had often streamed with the blood of the more active royalists: the spirits of many were broken with tedious imprisonments: the estates of all were burdened by the fines and confiscations which had been levied upon them: no one durst openly avow himself of that party: and so small did their number seem to a superficial view, that, even should the nation recover its liberty, which was now deemed nowise possible, it was uncertain what form of government it should embrace (p. 342). But amidst all these gloomy prospects, *fortune*,[8] by surprising revolution, was now paving the way for the king to mount, in peace and triumph, the throne of his ancestors (p. 342).

When Monk began to put his great project into execution, the nation had fallen into total anarchy. He advanced with his army, which was near six thousand men: the scattered forces in England were above five times more numerous. In all counties through which Monk passed, the prime gentry flocked to him with addresses, expressing their earnest desire that he would be instrumental in restoring the nation to peace and tranquillity, and to the enjoyment of those liberties which by law were their birthright, but of which, during so many years, they had been fatally bereaved

7. In 1659, a year before the Restoration! I bow before the will of the people.
8. No doubt!

(p. 352). Men were sent to confirm the general in his inclination to a free parliament (p. 353). The tyranny and anarchy which now equally oppressed the kingdom; the experience of past distractions, the dread of future convulsions, the indignation against military usurpation, all these motives had united every party and formed a tacit coalition between the royalists and Presbyterians. These last agreed that they had gone too far, and the lessons of experience finally recruited them with the rest of England in desiring the king's restoration, the only remedy for all these fatal evils (pp. 333, 353).[9]

Monk pretended not to favour these addresses (p. 353). How early he entertained designs for the king's restoration, we know not with certainty (p. 345). When he arrived in London, he told the parliament that he had been employed as an instrument of Providence for effecting their restoration (p. 354). He added that it was to the parliament itself to decide the summoning of a new assembly which might finally give contentment to the nation, and it was sufficient for the public security, if the fanatical party and the royalists were excluded; since the principles of these factions were destructive either of government or liberty (p. 355).

He even obeyed the Long Parliament in a violent measure (p. 356). But as soon as intelligence was conveyed of his decision for a new convocation, joy and exultation appeared throughout the kingdom. The royalists and Presbyterians mingled in common joy and transport to curse their tyrants (p. 358). All these motives united every party, except the most desperate (p. 353).[10]

9. In 1659. But four years earlier, the royalists, according to the same historian, foolishly miscalculated when they imagined that enemies of the government were friends of the king. See p. 242.

10. In 1660; but in 1655, 'they feared the restoration of the monarchy more than they hated the established government' (p. 209).

From a History by David Hume 189

Determined republicans, particularly the late king's judges, did not neglect their own interests in these circumstances. By themselves or their emissaries, they represented to the soldiers, that all those brave actions which had been performed during the war, and which were so meritorious in the eyes of the parliament, would be regarded as the deepest crimes by the royalists and would expose the army to the severest vengeance: that in vain did that party make professions of moderation and lenity; the king's death, the execution of so many nobility and gentry, the sequestration and imprisonment of the rest, were in the eyes of the royalists unpardonable crimes (p. 366).

But the agreement of all parties formed one of those popular torrents, where the most indifferent, or even the most averse, are transported with the general passion. The enthusiasts themselves seemed to be disarmed of their fury; suspended between despair and astonishment, they gave way to measures which they found it would be impossible to withstand (p. 363). The voice of the nation, without noise, *but with infinite ardour*, called for the king's restoration.[11] *The kingdom was still almost entirely in the hands of the republicans;*[12] and some among them began to renew demands for *conditions* and to recall old proposals: but the general opinion seemed to condemn all these capitulations with the sovereign. Harassed with convulsions and disorders, men were terrified at the mention of negotiations or delays. The passion too for liberty, having been carried to such violent extremes, began, by a natural movement, to give place to a spirit of loyalty and obedience.

11. But the preceding year, THE PEOPLE signed, *without hesitation*, an agreement to maintain the republic. Thus, it took only some 365 days for the heart of the Sovereign to change from *hate* or *indifference* to *infinite ardour*.

12. Note well!

After the legal concessions made by the late king, the constitution seemed to be sufficiently secured (p. 364).

The parliament, whose functions were about to expire, had voted that no one should be elected who had himself, or whose father, had borne arms for the late king (p. 365); for they knew that to call a free parliament, and to restore the royal family, were visibly, in the present disposition of the kingdom, one and the same measure (p. 361); but little regard was anywhere paid to this ordinance (p. 365).

Such was the turn affairs took in England, when . . .

Caetera DISIDERANTUR.

Postscript

The latest edition of this work was nearing completion when certain completely trustworthy Frenchmen assured me that the book *Développement des principes fondamentaux*, etc.,[1] which I cite in Chapter 8, contains maxims that the king does not approve.[2]

'The authors of the book in question', they tell me, 'are magistrates who reduce the right of the Estates-General to that of presenting grievances and attribute to the parlements the executive power of verifying all laws, even those which are the result of a request from the Estates, which is to say they elevate the magistracy above the nation.'

---

1. This is the third in five months, counting the pirated French edition that has just appeared. This last faithfully copied all the errors of the first, and added others as well.

2. [Maistre had received a letter from the count d'Avaray expressing the king's disapproval. See *Joseph de Maistre et Blacas*, ed. E. Daudet (Paris: Plan-Nourrit, 1908), p. 3.]

I avow that I had not perceived this monstrous error in their book (and which I do not share); this error even appeared to me to be excluded by certain of its texts, quoted on pages 115 and 116 of my work, and it can be seen by my note on page 115 that the book in question can give rise to objections of quite another sort.

If, as I am assured, the authors have deviated from true principles in reference to the legitimate rights of the French nation, I am not surprised that their work, otherwise full of excellent things, has alarmed the king, for even those persons who have never had the honour of meeting him know by a great many unimpeachable witnesses that these sacred rights have no more loyal protector than himself and that nothing would offend him more than the preaching of contrary systems.

I repeat that I read this book on the *Développement*, etc., with no systematic view. Long separated from my books, obliged to use those that I found rather than those I would have preferred, often reduced to citing from memory, I needed a collection of this kind to collect my ideas. It was recommended to me (I must say it) by the stand it took against the monarchy's enemies. But if it contains errors that I overlooked, I sincerely disavow them. Alien to all systems, all parties, and all hatreds by both reflexion and position, I will assuredly be most satisfied if every reader will read me with intentions as pure as those that dictated my work.

In conclusion, if I wanted to study the character of the different powers under the old French constitution, if I wanted to go back to the source of all these questions and develop clear ideas on the essence, function, rights, complaints, and wrongs of the parlement, I would go beyond the bounds of a postscript, or of my book even, and moreover, I would be undertaking a perfectly useless task. If the French nation recovers its king, as every friend of order must hope, and if there are regular national assemblies, the various powers will naturally find their places without contradictions or difficulties. Whatever the case, the exaggerated claims of the parlements, the discussion and quarrels to which they gave birth, all appear to me to be entirely a matter of ancient history.

Suggestions for Additional Reading

The standard edition of Maistre's writings is the *Oeuvres complètes* in fourteen volumes (Lyons: 1884–93). Unfortunately this edition is far from complete. The most important omissions are his journal, *Les Carnets du comte Joseph de Maistre*, edited by X. de Maistre (Lyons: Vitte, 1923); *La Franc-Maçonnerie: Mémoire inédit au duc de Brunswick*, edited by E. Dermenghem (Paris: Rieder, 1925); *Mémoires politiques et correspondance diplomatique*, edited by A. Blanc (Paris: 1858); *Correspondance diplomatique, 1811–1817*, edited by A. Blanc (Paris: 1860); and *Joseph de Maistre et Blacas: Leur correspondance inédite et l'histoire de leur amitié*, edited by E. Daudet (Paris: Plan-Nourrit, 1908). There is an excellent English translation of Maistre's *Essai sur le principe générateur des constitutions politiques et des autres institutions humaines* published under the title *On God and Society*, edited by Elisha Greifer and translated with the assistance of Lawrence M. Porter (Chicago: Henry Regnery Co., 1959). *The Works of Joseph de Maistre* (New York: Macmillan, 1965) provides translated selections from some of Maistre's most important works (but without critical notes) and a lucid general introduction by the editor, Jack Lively.

There is a considerable literature in French on Joseph de Maistre. The most recent and most complete study is Robert Triomphe's *Joseph de Maistre: Etude sur la vie et sur la doctrine d'un matérialiste mystique* (Geneva: Droz, 1968). Triomphe's book also provides a valuable listing of all Maistre's writings as well as a complete and annotated bibliography of the secondary literature in French, English, German, Italian, and Russian. The only easily available book-length study of Maistre in English is Richard A. Lebrun's *Throne and Altar: The Political and Religious Thought of Joseph de Maistre* (Ottawa: University of Ottawa, 1965). There is an excellent chapter on Maistre in Paul H. Beik's *The French Revolution Seen from the Right: Social Theories in Motion, 1789–1799* (Philadelphia: American Philosophical Society, 1956). The following articles may also be consulted: John Courtney Murray, 'Political Thought of Joseph de Maistre', *Review of Politics* 11: 63–86, January 1949; Elisha Greifer, 'Joseph de Maistre and the Reaction against the Eighteenth Century', *American Political Science Review* 15: 591–98, September 1961; and Richard Lebrun, 'Joseph de Maistre, Cassandra of Science', *French Historical Studies* 6: 214–31, Fall 1969.

Beik's above-mentioned study remains the best general introduction to French counter-revolutionary writers. Jacques Godechot's *The Counter-Revolution: Doctrine and Action, 1789–1804* (New York: Howard Fertig, 1971) includes English and German writers and thus provides broader coverage, but his treatment of French authors adds nothing to Beik. Readers will, of course, want to study Joseph de Maistre in the context of the Enlightenment and the French Revolution. The literature on these latter topics is too vast and easily available to require comment here.

Index

Henry VIII (of England), 120n
Hereditary monarchy, precious character of, 120
Herodotus, 38
Heroides (Ovid), 99
Histoire ecclésiastique (C. F. Fleury), 117
History: as experimental politics, 16, 65–66, 108, 167; red with blood, 53
History of Dahomey (Dalzel), 51
History of England (Hume), 16, 68n, 92n, 119n, 171–91
History of the Rebellion and Civil War in England (Clarendon), 168
Holland, 46
Honour, gift of God or the sovereign, 105
Homer, 85, 96, 72, 159
Horace, 60n, 145, 150n
Human blood. *See* bloodshed
Human freedom, and the Supreme Being, 23
Human legislation. *See* legislator
Human reason, essentially disruptive, 13, 80
Human soul, and bloodshed, 58
Hume, David: and Maistre, 4, 16–17; as political theorist, 96; cited, 68n, 92n, 119n, 168, 171–95

Icon Animorum (Barclay), 107
Iliad (Homer), 104
'Illuminism': and Maistre, 3, 46n; described, 3

Immorality, and impermanence, 12
Independents, 172
Ingolsby, Richard, 157
Innocence: and prejudice, 33; and suffering, 61–62
Innovation, 93
Institutions: deification of, 13, 80–85; and the Divinity, 14; and written laws, 93; fragility if manmade, 103–4; of the French Republic, 144
Iphigénie (Racine), 33
Irreligion: as cause of the Revolution, 1; and Freemasonry, 12; as the 'anathema' of the Republic, 12
Isaias, 137
Ishmael, son of, 80, 83
Islam: deified institutions, 13, 80, 83; its warlike record, 54–55

Jacobins, 10, 17, 102n
James II (of England), 146, 151
Janus, temple of, 51, 53
Jerusalem Delivered (Tasso), 75
Jesuits, possibility of reestablishment, 82
Joan of Arc, 136
Johannet, R. de, vii
Joseph II (of Austria), 58n
Journal de l'opposition, 74
Judaism, 13, 80
Julian the Apostate, 87–88
Jupiter, 159
Justice, and the old French constitution, 116

Personnel of the Directory, and restoration, 152
Philip of Valois, 56
Philippe Egalité, duke of Orléans, 33n
Philosophes, 4
Philosophism, 13, 85, 88–89, 164n
Philosophy: essentially disruptive, 13, 80; of the eighteenth century, 103
Philosophical optimism, 62n
Physicists, and divine justice, 32
Piedmont-Sardinia, 2, 18
Pisistratids, 94
Pitt, William, 25n
Plan for a Perfect Republic, imagined work of Hume, 96
Plato, 61n, 67, 87, 96n
Platonism, 3
Pliny the Younger, 85
Plutarch, 67n, 94n, 203n
Political theory, and constitutional law, 95
Political reform, and Freemasonry, 3
Popular sovereignty, 12
Portugal, 185
Positions, under republics and monarchies, 147–50
Prejudices, and guilt, 33
Presbyterianism, 45
Presbyterians, 179, 189
Pride, and political judgment, 24
Priests, in French government, 112–13
Principi d'una Scienza nuova (Vico), 163n
Probability, laws of, 12, 66

Prometheus, 104
Property of the nation, 16, 152–55
Protestant churches, 47
Protestant nations, 46, 83
Protestant Reformation, 57
Proverbs, 48
Providence: and the French Revolution, 1, 6, 10–11, 26–30, 31–50, 130, 158; and Freemasonry, 3; character of its action, 32, 38–39, 46, 59, 140–42, 167; and France, 47, 130, 136–37; and political constitutions, 93–94, 134–35
Providential interpretation of the Revolution, 6–7
Public opinion: and Louis XVIII, 127–28; in a monarchy, 158–59
Puritan Commonwealth, see Commonwealth

Quiberon expedition, 25n, 139, 149
Quotidienne, 100n

Racine, Jean-Baptiste, 33, 96, 119
Racine (the younger), 113
Raft of the Medusa (Géricault), 11
Rank, in France, 105
Rationalism: and Freemasonry, 3; and Maistre's *Lettres d'un royaliste savoisien*, 6
Reason, 129–30
Rebirth, as theme, 11
Redemption, and bloodshed, 11, 58–63

Reflections on the Revolution in France (Burke), 5
Regicide, 36, 158
Reign of Terror, 8, 13, 16, 27, 143
Religion: and the Revolution, 1, 18; and lasting institutions, 12–13, 80–85, 94; and the nobility, 163n
Religious orders, 62
Representation: and mandates, 70; and sovereignty, 71–72
Representative government: its feudal origins, 12, 67–68; and France, 12, 65, 70–73; and England, 67–70; and America, 70
Republican government: and virtue, 12, 74; and France, 12
Restoration of the French monarchy: possible in 1797, 8; and the church, 14, 141; prophesied, 16, 131–37; and Maistre, 18–19; and peace, 42–43; and the French, 131, 133, 135–37; and God, 141
Reunion of the Christian churches, 3
Revolution: and the papacy, 17; and conquest, 107; and counter-revolution, 139, 167; laws of, 161
Revolutionary chariot, 28
Revolutionary periods, characteristics of, 24–25
Richelieu, Cardinal, 184
Rights: of the nobility, 2; of God, 91–95; of monarchs, 92; of the people, 92

Robespierre, Maximilien: and Cult of the Supreme Being, 13; and the Reign of Terror, 27, 32, 38, 126–27, 143; genius of, 41, 107; and the priesthood, 79; quoted, 178n
Roman Catholicism, 17
Roman people, and Caesar, 135
Roman republic, 65
Roman world, ruins of, 1
Romans, Epistle to (St. Paul), 62
Romanticism, 11
Rome, 46
Rousseau, Jean Baptiste, 61
Rousseau, Jean-Jacques, 4, 7, 9, 13, 59n, 71, 80, 104, 113n, 163n
Royal law, 115
Royal prerogatives, under the old French constitution, 114
Royalism, 5–6
Russia, and Maistre, 18–19

Sacrifice, 61–62
St. Benedict, 83
St. Ignatius, 82
St. John, 83
Saint-Leger, Bishop, 112
St. Martin, 83
Saint-Ouen, Bishop, 112
St. Paul, 62, 104
St. Petersburg, 18–19
Saint-Pierre, M. de, 162
Salon, constitution of, 94
Santerre, Antoine-Joseph, 34
Sardinia, 18
Savoy, house of, 2, 5–6
Savoy, province of, 2, 5

Sceptics, addressed on sociological level, 13, 80–84
Scholars, as legislators, 95
Scottish Rite Masons of the Strict Observance, 3
Seigneurial dues, in Savoy, 2
Self-denial Ordinance, 172
Self-sacrifice, 61–62
Senate of Savoy, 2
September Massacres, 45n
Septembrists, and Providence, 27
Shakespeare, William, 39, 119
Ship money, 177
Sidney, Algernon, 92n
Siméon, Joseph-Jérôme, 105
Social reform, and Freemasonry, 3
Sovereignty: and representative government, 12, 72, 147; crimes against, 34–35; and the Directory, 103; and monarchy, 147; and moral force, 159
Spain, 185
Sparta, 47, 67, 93, 118
Stael, Mme de, 7
Stuarts, 150
Subjectivism, 11
Subversive ideas, and the French Revolution, 18
Suleiman the Magnificent, 57
Sulla, 53
Supreme Being, and man, 9–10, 23
Sweden, 185
Switzerland, and Maistre, 5, 7–8

Talleyrand-Périgord, Charles Maurice de, 33n

Tallien, Jean Lambert, 27n
Tamerlane, 56
Tarquinius, 32, 94
Tasso, 75
Taxes, and French constitution, 116, 122
Temple of Janus, 51
Terror, Reign of. *See* Reign of Terror
Thouret, Jacques Guillaume, 37
Titus, Roman emperor, 53
Titus Livy, 94n, 122
Theodicy, and *Les Soirées de Saint-Pétersbourg*, 19
Theological vocabulary, and Maistre, 14
Theoretic nature of the old French constitution, 112
Thermidor, ninth of, 127
Throne and altar, and Maistre, 2
Tiberius, Roman emperor, 126
Totila, 54
Trial by jury, feudal origins of, 68; in France, 68; in England, 68
Turenne, Henri de la Tour d'Auvergne, 27n
Turin, and Maistre, 2, 19
Turin, government, and Maistre, 5

Ultraroyalists, and Maistre, 165n
United Provinces of the Netherlands, 185

Vaucanson, Jacques de, 28, 104
Venality of office, 117n
Vendémiaire uprising, 126